Among the Trees at Elmridge

by Ella Rodman

CONTENTS.

CHAPTER I.

A SPRING OPENING.

On that bright spring afternoon when three happy, interested children went off to the woods with their governess to take their first lesson in the study of wild flowers, they saw also some other things which made a fresh series of "Elmridge Talks," and these things were found among the trees of the roadside and forest.

"What makes it look so yellow over there, Miss Harson?" asked Clara, who was peering curiously at a clump of trees that seemed to have been touched with gold or sunlight. "And just look over here," she continued, "at these pink ones!"

Malcolm shouted at the idea:

"Yellow and pink trees! That sounds like a Japanese fan. Where are they, I should like to know?"

"Here, you perverse boy!" said his governess as she laughingly turned him around. "Are you looking up into the sky for them? There is a clump of golden willows right before you, with some rosy maples on one side. What other colors can you call them?"

Malcolm had to confess that "yellow and pink trees" were not so wide of the mark, after all, and that they were very pretty. Little Edith was particularly delighted with them, and wanted to "pick the flowers" immediately.

"They are too high for that, dear," was the reply, "and these blossoms--for that is what they really are, although nothing more than fringes and catkins-- are much prettier massed on the trees than they would be if gathered. The still-bare twigs and branches seem, as you see, to be draped with golden and rose-colored veils, but there will be no leaves until these queer flowers have dropped. If we look closely at the twigs and branches, we shall see that they are glossy and polished, as though they had been varnished and then brightened with color by the painter's brush. It is the flowing of the sap that does this. The swelling of the bark occasioned by the flow of sap gives the whole mass a livelier hue; hence the ashen green of the poplar, the golden green of the willow and the dark crimson of the peach tree, the wild rose and the red osier are perceptibly heightened by the first warm days of spring."

"Miss Harson," asked Clara, with a perplexed face, "what are catkins?"

"Here," said her governess, reaching from the top bar of the road-fence for the lowest branch of a willow tree; "examine this catkin for yourself, and I will tell you what my Botany says of it: 'An ament, or catkin, is an assemblage of flowers composed of scales and stamens or pistils arranged along a common thread-like receptacle, as in the chestnut and willow. It is a kind of calyx, by some classed as a mode of inflorescence (or flowering), and each chaffy scale protects one or more of the stamens or pistils, the whole forming one aggregate flower. The ament is common to forest-trees, as the oak and chestnut, and is also found upon the willow and poplar.'"

"It's funny-looking," said Malcolm, when he had made himself thoroughly acquainted with the appearance of the catkin, "but it doesn't look much like a flower: it looks more like a pussy's tail."

"Yes, and that is the origin of its name. 'Catkin' is diminutive for 'cat;' so this collection of flowers is called 'catkin,' or 'little cat.'"

"I think I'll call them 'pussy-tails,'" said Edith.

"There is a great deal to be learned about trees," said Miss Harson, when all were comfortably seated in the pleasant schoolroom; "and, besides the natural history of their species, some old trees have wonderful stories connected with them, while many in tropical countries are so wonderful in themselves that they do not need stories to make them interesting. The common trees around us will be our subjects at first; for I suppose that you can scarcely tell a willow from a poplar, or a chestnut tree from either, can you?"

"I can tell a chestnut tree," said Malcolm, confidently.

"When it is not the season for nuts?" asked his governess, smiling.

There was not a very positive reply to this; and Miss Harson continued:

"I do not think that any of us know as much as we ought to know of the trees which we see every day, and of the uses to which many of them are put, to say nothing of many familiar trees that we read about, and even depend upon for some of the necessaries of life."

"Like the cocoanut tree," suggested Clara.

"That is not exactly necessary to our comfort, dear," was the reply, "for people can manage to live without cocoanuts, although in many forms they are very agreeable to the taste, and it is only the inhabitants of the countries where they grow who look upon these trees as necessaries; but we will take them up in their turn. And first let us find out what we can about the willow, because it is the first tree, with us, to become green in the spring, and, of that large class which is called deciduous, the last one to lose its leaves."

"And why are they called deciduous?" asked Malcolm.

"Because they shed their leaves every autumn and are furnished with a new set in the spring: 'deciduous' is Latin for 'falling off.' And this is the case with nearly all our native trees and plants. Persistent, or permanent, leaves remain on the stem and branches all through the changes of season, like the leaves of the pine and box, while evergreens look fresh through the entire year and are generally cone-bearing and resinous trees. 'These change their leaves annually, but, the young leaves appearing before the old ones decay, the tree is always green.'"

"Miss Harson," said Clara, "when people talk about weeping willows, what do they mean? Do the trees really cry? I sometimes read about 'em in stories, and I never knew what they did."

"They cry dreadfully," said Malcolm, "when it rains."

"But only as you do when you are out in it," replied his governess--"by having the water drip from your clothes.--No, Clara, the tree is called 'weeping' because it seems to 'assume the attitude of a person in tears, who bends over and appears to droop.' The sprays of this tree are particularly beautiful, and 'willowy' is often used for 'graceful,' as meaning the same thing. Its language is 'sorrow,' and it is often seen in burial-grounds and in mourning-pictures. 'We remember it in sacred history, associating it with the rivers of Babylon, and with the tears of the children of Israel, who sat down under the shade of this tree and hung their harps upon its branches. It is distinguished by the graceful beauty of its outlines, its light-green, delicate foliage, its sorrowing attitude and its flowing drapery.'"

"Were those weeping willows that we saw to-day?" asked Clara.

"No," replied her brother, quickly; "they just stuck up straight and didn't weep a bit."

"They are called water willows," said Miss Harson, "because they are never found in dry places. They are more common than the weeping willow. The water willow has the same delicate foliage and the same habit, under an April sky, of gleaming with a drapery of golden verdure among the still-naked trees of the forest or orchard. 'When Spring has closed her delicate flowers,' says a bright writer, 'and the multitudes that crowd around the footsteps of May have yielded their places to the brighter host of June, the willow scatters the golden aments that adorned it, and appears in the deeper garniture of its own green foliage.' A group of these golden willows, seen in a rainstorm, will have so bright an appearance as to make it seem as if the sun were actually shining."

"I wish we had them all around here, then," said Edith; "I like to see the sun shining when it rains."

"But the sun is not shining, dear," replied her governess: "it is only the reflection from the willows that makes it look so; and we can make just such sunshine ourselves when it rains, or when there is dullness of any sort, by being all the more cheerful and striving to make others happy. Who loves to be called 'Little Sunshine'?"

"I do," said the child, caressing the hand that had patted her rosy cheek.

"Let's all be golden willows," said Malcolm, in a comical way that made them laugh.

Miss Harson told him that he could not make a better attempt than to be one of those home-brighteners who bring the sunshine with them, but she added that such people are always considerate for others. Malcolm wondered a little if this meant that he was not, but he soon forgot it in hearing the many things that were to be said of the willow.

"The family-name of this tree is Salix, from a word that means 'to spring,' because a willow-branch, if planted, will take root and grow so quickly that it seems almost like magic. 'And they shall spring up as among the grass, as willows by the watercourses,' says the prophet Isaiah, speaking of the children of the people of God. The flowers of the willow are of two kinds--one bearing stamens, and the other pistils--and each grows upon a separate plant. When the ovary, at the base of the pistil, is ripe, it opens by two valves and lets out, as through a door, multitudes of small seeds covered with a fine down, like the seeds of the cotton-plant. This downy substance is greedily sought after by the birds as a lining for their nests, and they may be seen carrying it away in their bills. And in some parts of Germany people take the trouble to collect it and use it as a wadding to their winter dresses, and even manufacture it into a coarse kind of paper."

"What queer people!" exclaimed Clara. "And how funny they must look in their wadded dresses!"

"They are not graceful people," was the reply, "but they live in a cold climate and show their good sense by dressing as warmly as possible. It was quite a surprise, though, to me to find that the willow was of use in clothing people. The more we learn of the works of God, the better we shall understand that last verse of the first chapter of the Bible: 'And God saw everything that he had made, and behold, it was very good.' The bees, too, are attracted by the willow catkins, but they do not want the down. On mild days whole swarms of them may be seen reveling in the sweets of the fresh blossoms. 'Cold days will come long after the willow catkins appear, and the bees will find but few flowers venturesome enough to open their petals. They have, however, thoroughly enjoyed their feast, and the short season of plenty will often be the means of saving a hive from famine.'"

"Are willow baskets made of willow trees?" asked Malcolm.

"Yes," said Miss Harson. "Basket-making has been a great industry in England from the earliest times; the ancient Britons were particularly skillful in weaving the supple wands of the willow. They even made of these slender stems little boats called 'coracles,' in which they could paddle down the small rivers, and the boats could be carried on their shoulders when they were walking on dry land."

"Just like our Indians' birch-bark canoes," said Malcolm, who was reading about the North American Indians. "But isn't it strange, Miss Harson, that the Indians and the Britons didn't get drowned going out in such little light boats?"

"Their very lightness buoyed them up upon the waves," was the reply; "but it does seem wonderful that they could bear the weight of men. The willow, however, was also used by the Romans in making their battle-shields, and even for the manufacture of ropes as well as baskets. The rims of cart-wheels, too, used to be made of willow, as now they are hooped with iron; so, you see, it is a strong wood as well as a pliant one. The kind used for basket-making is the Salix viminalis, and the rods of this species are called 'osiers.' Let us see now what this English book says of the process of basket-making:

"'The quick and vigorous growth of the willow renders it easy to provide materials for this branch of industry. Osier-beds are planted in every suitable place, and here the willow-cutter comes as to an ample store. Autumn is the season for him to ply his trade, and he cuts the willow rods down and ties them in bundles. He then sets them up on end in standing water to the depth of a few inches. Here they remain during the winter, until the shoots, in the following spring, begin to sprout, when they are in a fit state to be peeled. A machine is used in some places to compress the greatest number of rods into a bundle.

"'Aged or infirm people and women and children can earn money by peeling willows at so much per bundle. The operation is very simple, and so is the necessary apparatus. Sometimes a wooden bench with holes in it is used, the willow-twigs being drawn through the holes. Another way is to draw the rod through two pieces of iron joined together, and with one end thrust into the ground to make it stand upright. The willow-peeler sits down before his instrument and merely thrusts the rod between the two pieces of iron and draws it out again. This proceeding scrapes the bark off one end, and then he turns it and fits it in the other way; so that by a simple process the whole rod is peeled. When the rods are quite prepared, they are again tied up in bundles and sold to the basket-makers.'"

"But how do they make the baskets?" asked Clara and Edith. "That is the nicest part."

"There is little to tell about it, though," said their governess, "because it is such easy work that any one can learn to do it. You saw the Indian women making baskets when papa took us to Maine last summer, and you noticed how very quickly they did it, beginning with the flat bottom and working rapidly up. It is a favorite occupation for the blind, and one of the things which are taught them in asylums."

"I wonder," said Malcolm, "if there is anything else that can be done with the willow?"

"Oh yes," replied Miss Harson; "we have not yet come to the end of its resources. It makes the best quality of charcoal, and in many parts of England the tree is raised for this express purpose. 'The abode of the charcoal-burner,' says an English writer, 'may be known from a distance by the cloud of smoke that hovers over it, and that must make it rather unhealthy. It is sometimes a small dome-shaped hut made of green turf, and, except for the difference of the material, might remind us of the hut of the Esquimaux. Beside it stands a caravan like those which make their appearance at fairs, and that contains the family goods and chattels. A string of clothes hung out to dry, a water-tub and a rough, shaggy dog usually complete the picture.'"

"But how can people live in the hut," asked Malcolm, "if the charcoal is burned in it? Ugh! I should think they'd choke."

"They certainly would," said his governess; "for the charcoal-smoke is death when inhaled for any length of time. But the charcoal-burner knows this quite as well as does any one else, and he makes his fire outside of the house, puts a rude fence around it and lets it smoke away like a huge pipe.

The hut is more or less enveloped in smoke, but this is not so bad as letting it rise from the inside would be. A great deal of willow charcoal is made in Germany and other parts of Europe."

"But, Miss Harson," said Clara, in a puzzled tone, "I don't see what they do with it all. It doesn't take much to clean people's teeth."

"No, dear," was the smiling reply, "and I am afraid that the people who make it are rather careless about their teeth.--You need not laugh, Malcolm, because it is 'just like a girl,' for it is quite as much like a boy not to know things which he has never been taught, and you must remember that you have two years the start of your sister in getting acquainted with the world. Perhaps you will kindly tell us of some of the uses to which charcoal is applied?"

"Well," said the young gentleman, after an awkward silence, "it takes lots of it to kindle fires."

"I do not think that Kitty ever uses it in the kitchen," said Miss Harson, "for she is supplied with kindling-wood for that purpose. You will have to think of something else."

But Malcolm could not think, and his governess finally told him that a great deal of charcoal is used for making gun-powder, and still more for fuel in France and the South of Europe, where a brass vessel supplies the place of a grate or stove. Quantities of it are consumed in steel-and iron-works, in preserving meat and other food, and in many similar ways. The children listened with great interest, and Malcolm felt sure that the next time he was asked about charcoal he would have a sensible answer.

"Our insect friends the aphides, or plant-lice, are very fond of the willow," continued Miss Harson, "and in hot, dry weather great masses of them gather on the leaves and drop a sugary juice, which the country-people call 'honey-dew,' and in some remote places, where knowledge is limited, it has been thought to come from the clouds. But we, who have learned something about these aphides[1], know that it comes from their little green bodies, and that the ants often carry the insects off to their nests, where they feed and 'tend them for the sake of this very juice. The aphis that infests the willow is the largest of the tribe, and the branches and stems of the tree are often blackened by the honey-dew that falls upon them."

[1] See Flyers and Crawlers, by the author. Presbyterian Board of Publication.

"Do willow trees grow everywhere?" asked Clara.

"They are certainly found in a great many different places," was the reply, "and even in the warmest countries. In one of the missionary settlements in Africa there is a solitary willow that has a story attached to it. It was the only tree in the settlement--think what a place that must have been!--except those the missionary had planted in his own garden, and it would never have existed but for the laziness of its owner. Nothing would have induced any of the natives to take the trouble to plant a tree, and therefore the willow had not been planted. But it happened, a long-time ago, that a native had fetched a log of wood from a distance, to make into a bowl when he should feel in the humor to do so. He threw the log into a pool of water, and soon forgot all about it. Weeks and months passed, and he never felt in the humor to work. But the log of wood set to work of its own accord. It had been cut from a willow, and it took root at the bottom of the pool and began to grow. In the end it became a handsome and flourishing tree."

This story was approved by the young audience, except that it was too short; but their governess laughingly said that, as there was nothing more to tell, it could not very well be any longer.

"The weeping willow," continued Miss Harson, "was first planted in England in not so lazy a way, but almost as accidentally. Many years ago a basket of figs was sent from Turkey to the poet Pope, and the basket was made of willow. Willows and their cousins the poplars are natives of the East; you remember that the one hundred and thirty-seventh psalm says of the captive Jews, 'By the rivers of Babylon, there we sat down, yea, we wept, when we remembered Zion. We hanged our harps upon the willows in the midst thereof.' 'The poet valued highly the small slender twigs, as associated with so much that was interesting, and he untwisted the basket and planted one of the branches in the ground. It had some tiny buds upon it, and he hoped he might be able to rear it, as none of this species of willow was known in England. Happily, the willow is very quick to take root and grow. The little branch soon became a tree, and drooped gracefully over the river in the same manner that its race had done over the waters of Babylon. From that one branch all the weeping willows in England are descended.'"

"And then they were brought over here," said Malcolm. "But what odd leaves they have, Miss Harson!--so narrow and long. They don't look like the leaves of other trees."

"The leaf is somewhat like that of the olive, only that of the olive is broader. The willow is a native of Babylon, and the weeping willow is called Salix Babylonica. It was considered one of the handsomest trees of the East, and is particularly mentioned among those which God commanded the Israelites to select for branches to bear in their hands at the feast of tabernacles. Read the verse, Malcolm--the fortieth of the twenty-third chapter of Leviticus."

Malcolm read:

"'And ye shall take you on the first day the boughs of goodly trees, branches of palm trees, and the boughs of thick trees, and willows of the brook; and ye shall rejoice before the Lord your God seven days.'"

"A place called the 'brook of the willows,'" added his governess, "is mentioned in Isaiah xv. 7, and this brook, according to travelers in Palestine, flows into the south-eastern extremity of the Dead Sea. The willow has always been considered by the poets as an emblem of woe and desertion, and this idea probably came from the weeping of the captive Jews under the willows of Babylon. The branches of the Salix Babylonica often droop so low as to touch the ground, and because of this sweeping habit, and of its association with watercourses in the Bible, it has been considered a very suitable tree to plant beside ponds and fountains in ornamental grounds, as well as in cemeteries as an emblem of mourning."

"How much there is to remember about the willow!" said Clara, thoughtfully. "I wonder if all the trees will be so interesting?"

"They are not all Bible trees," replied Miss Harson. "But the wise king of Israel found them interesting, for he 'spake of trees, from the cedar tree that is in Lebanon even unto the hyssop that springeth out of the wall.'"

CHAPTER II.

THE MAPLES.

"The pink trees next, I suppose," said Malcolm, "since we have had the yellow ones?"

"Real pink trees?" asked Edith, with very wide-open eyes.

"No, dear;" replied her governess; "there are no pink trees, except when they are covered with bloom like the peach trees. Malcolm only means the maples that we saw in blossom yesterday and thought of such a pretty color. There are many varieties of the maple, which is always a beautiful and useful tree, but the red, or scarlet, maple is the very queen of the family. It is not so large as are most of the others; but when a very young tree, its grace and beauty are noticeable among its companions. It is often found in low, moist places, but it thrives just as well in high, dry ground; and it is therefore a most convenient tree. Here is a very pretty description, Malcolm, in one of papa's large books, that you can read to us."

Malcolm read remarkably well for a boy of his age, and he always enjoyed being called upon in this way.

Miss Harson pointed to these lines:

"Coming forth in the spring, like morning in the east, arrayed in crimson and purple; bearing itself, not proudly but gracefully in modest green, among the more stately trees in summer; and ere it bids adieu to the season stepping forth in robes of gold, vermilion, crimson and variegated scarlet,-- stands the queen of the American forest, the pride of all eyes and the delight of every picturesque observer of nature, the red maple."

"Why, I never saw such a tree as that!" exclaimed Clara, in great surprise.

"Yes, dear," replied her governess; "you have seen it, but you never thought of describing it to yourself in just this way. When you saw it yesterday, it was coming forth in the spring, like morning in the east, arrayed in crimson and purple,' but you just called it a pink tree. It is much nearer red, however, than it is pink."

"I've seen all the rest of the colors, too," said Malcolm, "when we went out after nuts."

"That is its autumn dress," said Miss Harson, "although a small tree is often seen with no color on it but brilliant red. But first we must see what it is like in spring and summer. It is also called the scarlet, the white, the soft and the swamp maple, and the flowers, as you see from this specimen, are in whorls, or pairs, of bright crimson, in crowded bunches on the purple branches. The leaves are in three or five lobes, with deep notches between, and some of them are very broad, while others are long and narrow. The trunk of the red maple is a clear ashy gray, often mottled with patches of white lichens; and when the tree is old, the bark cracks and can be peeled off in long, narrow strips."

"Is anything done with the bark?" asked Clara.

"Yes, it is used, with other substances, for dyeing, and also for making ink. The sap, too, can be boiled down to sugar, but it is not nearly so rich as that of the proper sugar-maple. The wood, which is very light-colored with a tinge of rose in it, is often made into common furniture, as it takes a fine polish and is easy to work with. It is used, too, for building-purposes. The early-summer foliage of the red maple is of a beautiful yellow green, and the young leaves are very delicate and airy-looking; but the graceful tree is in such a hurry to display her gay autumn colors that she will often put on a scarlet or crimson streamer in July or August. One brilliantly-colored branch will be seen on a green tree, or the leaves of an entire tree will turn red while all the other trees around it are clothed in summer greenness."

"Don't you remember, Miss Harson," said Edith, "the little tree that I thought was on fire and how frightened I was?"

"Yes, dear, I remember it very well--an innocent little red maple that would put on its flame-colored dress when it should have been all in green, like its sisters; but it was too green at heart to be in a blaze. This tree is often used for fuel, but it has to be cut down and dried first. The reddening of the leaf generally begins at the veins and spreads out from them until the whole is tinted. Sometimes it appears in spots, almost like drops of blood, on the green surface; but, come as it will, it is always beautiful. It is said of the red maple that 'it stands among the occupants of the forest like Venus among the planets--the brightest in the midst of brightness and the most beautiful in a constellation of beauty,'"

"Is there such a thing as a silver tree?" asked Clara.

"There is a tree called 'the silver maple,'" was the reply, "and there is also the silver poplar. The silver maple is considered the most graceful of the large and handsome maple family. I have not told you, I think, that the name of the family is Acer, which means 'sharp' or 'hard,' and it was supposed to have been given in old English times when the wood of the maple was used for javelins. The silver maple gets its name from the whitish under-surface of its leaves, and it is a favorite shade-tree; it has a slender trunk and long, drooping branches. The foliage is light and rather dull-looking, and it is not a very bright tree in autumn. The leaves are so deeply notched that they have a fringe-like appearance, and this, with its slender form and bending, swaying habit, gives it a very graceful look."

Little Edith wished to know "if the wood was like silver," and Malcolm asked her how she expected it to grow if it was.

But Miss Harson replied kindly,

"The silver, dear, is all in the leaves, and there is not much of it there. The wood is white and of little use, as it is soft and perishable; but the beauty of the finely-cut foliage, the contrast between the green of the upper surface of the leaves and the silver color of the lower, and the magnificent spread of the limbs of the white maple, recommend it as an ornamental tree; and this is the purpose for which it is intended. It is used very largely in the cities for shade and beauty. It is often called the 'river maple,' because it is so frequently seen on the banks of streams."

"And now," said Malcolm, "I hope there is ever so much about the maple-sugar tree. Can't we get some this spring, Miss Harson, before it's all gone?"

"We can certainly buy the sugar in town, Malcolm, if that is what you mean; but it does not grow on the trees in cakes, and we shall scarcely be able to tap the trunks and go through with the process of preparing the sap, even if it were not too late for that. We will do what we can, though, to become acquainted with the rock maple, that we may be able to recognize it when we see it. When young, it is a beautiful, neat and shapely tree with a rich, full leafy head of a great variety of forms. It is the largest and strongest of the maples, and gives the best shade. It can be distinguished from the other members of the family by its leaves, in which the notch between the lobes is round instead of being sharp, and also by their appearing at the same time with the blossoms, which are of a yellowish-green color. The green tint of the leaves is darker on some trees than it is on others, and in autumn they become, often before the first touch of the frost, of a splendid orange or gold, sometimes of a bright scarlet or crimson, color, each tree commonly retaining from year to year the same color or colors, and differing somewhat from every other. The most beautiful and valuable maple-wood is taken from this tree. It is known as 'curled maple' and 'bird's-eye maple,' and the common variety looks like satin-wood. In the curled maple the fibres are in waves instead of in straight lines, and the surface seems to change with alternate light and shade; in the bird's-eye, irregular snarls of fibres look like roundish projections rising from hollow places, each one resembling the eye of a bird. Buckets, tubs and many useful things are made of the straight variety, and for lasts it is considered better than any other kind of wood. The curled and the bird's-eye are largely used for furniture."

"But isn't it a shame," said Clara, "to spoil the maple-sugar by making the trees into chairs and things?"

"You would not think so," replied her governess, "if you needed the 'chairs and things' more than you need the sugar. But the supply of trees seems to be sufficient for both purposes."

"Does the sugar come right out of the tree when people tap on it with a hammer?" asked Edith, whose ideas of sugar-making were rather crude.

"You blessed baby!" cried Malcolm, with a shout of laughter. Let's take our hammers and go after some maple-sugar right away."

"No, Edie," said Miss Harson as she took her much-loved little pupil on her lap; "we'll stay at home and learn just how the sugar is made. To tap a tree, dear, means to make cuts in the trunk for the sap to flow out, and in the sugar-maple this sap is more like water than sugar. From the middle of February to the second week in March, according to the warmth or the coldness of the locality, is the time for tapping the trees; and when the holes are bored, spouts of elder or sumac from which the pith has been taken are put into them at one end, while the other goes down to the bucket which receives the sap. 'Several holes are so bored that their spouts shall lead to the same bucket, and high enough to allow the bucket to hang two or three feet from the ground, to prevent leaves and dirt from being blown in.' The next thing is to boil the sap, and this is done in great iron kettles, over immense wood-fires, out there among the trees, with plenty of snow on the ground, and only two or three rude little cabins for the men and boys to sleep in. This is called 'the sugar-camp,' and the sap-season lasts five or six weeks."

"And why is it boiled?"

"Boiling drives the water off in vapor, and leaves the sugar behind in the pot."

"And do they stay in the woods there all the time?" asked Malcolm, with great interest. "What lots of fun they must have, with the big fires and the snow and as much maple-sugar as ever they want to eat! I'd like to stay in a sugar-camp in the woods."

"Perhaps not, after trying it and finding how much hard work there is in sugar-making," replied his governess. "'The kettles must be carefully watched and plenty of wood brought to keep them boiling, and during the process the sap, or syrup, is strained; lime or salaeratus is added, to neutralize the free acid; and the white of egg, isinglass or milk, to cause foreign substances to rise in a scum to the surface. When it has been sufficiently boiled, the syrup is poured into moulds or casks to harden.' The sugar with which the most pains have been taken is very light-colored, and I have seen it almost white."

"Have you ever been to a sugar-camp, Miss Harson?" asked Clara, who was wishing, like Malcolm, that she could go to one herself.

"Yes," said Miss Harson; "I did go once, in Vermont, when the family with whom I was staying took me to see the 'sugaring off.' This is putting it into the pans and buckets to harden after it has been sufficiently boiled and clarified; and we younger ones, by way of amusement, were allowed to make jack-wax."

"Oh!" exclaimed three voices at once; "what is that? Is it good to eat?"

"I thought it particularly good," was the reply, "and I am quite sure that you would agree with me. To make it, we poured a small quantity of hot syrup on the snow to cool; and when it was fit to eat, it was just like wax, instead of being hard like the cakes in moulds. It took only a few minutes, too, to make it, and it seemed a great deal nicer because we did it ourselves. I remember that it was the last of March and very cold, but there were big fires to get warmed at, and we had a delightful time."

"Were there any Indians there, Miss Harson?" asked little Edith, after being quiet for some time. Vermont was such a long way off on the map, besides being up almost at the top, that Indians and bears and all sorts of wild things seemed to have a right to live there.

"No," said her governess, smiling at the question; "I did not see one, even at the sugar-camp. Yet the Indians made maple-sugar long before we knew anything about it, and from them the white people learned how to do it."

"Well, that's the funniest thing!" exclaimed Malcolm. "I thought that Indians were always scalping people instead of making maple-sugar."

"They did a great many other things, though, besides fighting, and their life was spent so much out of doors that they studied the nature of every plant and living thing about them. The healing-properties of some of our most valuable herbs were first discovered by the Indians, and, as they never had any grocery-stores, the presence of trees that would supply them with sugar was a blessing not likely to be neglected. The devoted missionary John Brainerd first heard of this tree-sugar from them, and it is said that he used to preach to them when they were thus peacefully employed, and obtained a better hearing than at other times."

"Have we any maple-sugar trees?" asked Clara.

"No," replied Miss Harson; "there are none at Elmridge, and I have seen none anywhere near here. They seem to flourish best in the Northern and North-eastern States, while in Western Canada the tree is found in groves of from five to twenty acres. These are called 'sugar-bushes,' and few farmers in that part of America are without them. In England the maple trees are called 'sycamores,' and the sap is used as a sweet drink. I will read to you from a little English book called Voices from the Woodlands a simple account of a country festival where maple sap was the choicest refreshment:

"'"Take care of that young tree," said Farmer Robinson to his laborer, who was diligently employed in clearing away a rambling company of brambles which had grown unmolested during the time of the last tenant; "the soil is good, and in a very few years we shall have pasturage for our bees, and plenty of maple-wine."

"'The farmer spoke true; before his young laborer had attained middle age the sapling had grown into a fine tree. Its branches spread wide and high, and bees came from all parts to gather their honey-harvests among the flowers; beneath its shade lambkins were wont in spring to sleep beside their dams; and when the time of shearing came, and the sheep were disburdened of their fleeces, you might see them hastening to the sycamore tree for shelter.

"'A kind of rustic festival was held about the same time in honor of the maple-wine. Hither came the farmer and his dame, with their children and young neighbors, each carrying bunches of flowers. Older people came in their holiday dresses, some with baskets containing cakes, others tea and sugar, with which the farmer and his wife had plentifully supplied them; and joyfully did they rest a while on the green sward while young men gathered sticks, and, a bright fire having been kindled, the kettle sent up its bubbling steam.

"'When this was ended, and few of the piled-up cakes remained--when, also, the young children had emptied their cans and rinsed them at the old stone trough into which rushed a full stream--tiny hands joyfully held up the small cans and bright eyes looked anxiously to the stem of the tall tree while the farmer warily cut an incision in the bark.

"'What joy when a sweet watery juice began to trickle! and the farmer filled one small cup, then another, till all were satisfied and a portion sent to the older people, who were contentedly looking on from the grassy slope where they had seated themselves. The farmer's wife knew naught concerning the process for obtaining sugar, or else she might have sweetened her children's puddings from the watery liquid yielded by the sycamore, or greater maple--an art well known to the aboriginal tribes of North America.'"

"Does that mean Indians, Miss Harson?" asked Malcolm, with a wry face at the long word.

"Yes," was the reply; "and I hope that you will feel properly grateful to these aborigines whenever you eat maple-sugar."

CHAPTER III.

OLD ACQUAINTANCES: THE ELMS.

Miss Harson had admonished her little flock that they must use their own eyes and be able to tell her things instead of depending altogether on her to tell them; so now they were all peering curiously among the trees to see which were putting on their new spring suits. The yellow trees and the pink trees had been readily distinguished, but, although the others had not been idle, it was not so easy for little people to discern their leaf-buds.

Clara soon made a discovery, however, of what her governess had noticed for a day or two, and the wonder was found on their own home-elms, those stately trees which had shaded the house ever since it was built, and from which the place got its pretty name--Elmridge.

"Well, dear," said Miss Harson, coming to the upper window from which an eager head was thrust, "what is it that you wish me to see?"

"Those funny flowers on the bare elm trees," was the reply. "Look, Miss Harson! Didn't I see them first?"

"You have certainly spoken of them first, for neither Malcolm nor Edith has said anything about them. But they must both come up here now, where they can see them, and Malcolm and I can manage to reach some of the blossoms by getting out of the broad window on to the little balcony."

Up came the two children kangaroo-fashion in a series of jumps, and presently Miss Harson was holding a cluster of dark maroon-colored flowers in her hand.

"How queer and dark they make the trees look!" said Malcolm; "and they're so thick that they 'most cover up the branches. They're like fringe."

"A very good description," replied his governess. "And now I wish you all to examine the trees very thoroughly and tell me afterward what you have noticed about them; then we will go down to the schoolroom and see what the books will tell us in our talk about the American elm and its cousin of England."

The books had a great deal to tell about them, but Miss Harson preferred to hear the children first.

"What did my little Edith see when she looked out of the window?" she asked.

"Stems of trees," was the reply, "with flowers on 'em."

"A very good general idea," continued Miss Harson, "but perhaps Clara can tell us something more particular about the elms?"

"They are very tall," said Clara, hesitatingly, "and they make it nice and shady in summer; and some of the branches bend over in such a lovely way! Papa calls one of them 'the plume.'"

"And now Malcolm?"

"The trunk--or big 'stem,' as Edie would call it--is very thick, and the branches begin low down, near the ground."

"Some of them do," said his governess, "but many of the elms on your father's grounds are seventy feet high before the branches begin. Sometimes two or three trunks shoot up together and spread out at the top in light, feathery plumes like palm trees. The elm has a great variety of shapes; sometimes it is a parasol, when a number of branches rise together to a great height and spread out suddenly in the shape of an umbrella. This makes a very regular-looking and beautiful tree. For about three-quarters of the way up, the 'plume' of which Clara speaks has one straight trunk, which then bends over droopingly. Small twigs cluster around the trunk all the way from bottom to top and give the tree the appearance of having a vine twining about it. I think that the plume-shape is the prettiest and most odd-looking of all the elms. Another strange shape is the vase, which seems to rest on the roots that stand out above the ground. 'The straight trunk is the neck of the vase, and the middle consists of the lower part of the branches as they swell outward with a graceful curve, then gradually diverge until they bend over at their extremities and form the lip of the vase by a circle of terminal sprays.'"

"Have we any trees that look like vases, Miss Harson?" asked Clara.

"Yes," was the reply; "not far from Hemlock Lodge there is one which we will look at when the leaves are all out. But you must not expect to find a perfect vase-shape, for it is only an approach to it. The dome-shaped elm has a broad, round head, which is formed by the shooting forth of branches of nearly equal length from the same part of the trunk, which gradually spread outward with a graceful curve into the roof or dome that crowns the tree."

"I know something else about our elms," said Malcolm: "some of the roots are on top of the ground. Isn't that very queer, Miss Harson?"

"Not for old elm trees, as this is quite a habit with them. Indeed, in many ways, the elm is so entirely different from other trees that it can be recognized at a great distance. It is both graceful and majestic, and is the most drooping of the drooping trees, except the willow, which it greatly surpasses in grandeur and in the variety of its forms. The green leaves are broad, ovate, heart-shaped, from two to four or five inches long. You can see their exact shape in this illustration. Their summer tint is very bright and vivid, but it turns in autumn to a sober brown, sometimes touched with a bright golden yellow, And now," continued Miss Harson, "we will examine the flowers which we have here, and we see that each blossom is on a green, slender thread less than half an inch long, and that it consists of a brown cup parted into seven or eight divisions, rounded at the border and containing about eight brown stamens and a long compressed ovary surmounted by two short styles. This ripens into a flattened seed-vessel before the leaves are fully out, and the seeds, being small and chaffy, are wafted in all directions and carried to great distances by the wind."

"Where does slippery elm come from?" asked Clara.

"From another American species, dear, which is very much like the white elm that we have been considering. The slippery elm is a smaller tree, does not droop so much, and the trunk is smoother and darker. The leaves are thicker and very rough on the upper side. The inner bark contains a great deal of mucilage--that, I suppose, is the reason for its being called 'slippery'--and it has been extensively used as a medicine. The wood is very strong and preferred to that of the white elm for building-purposes, although the latter is considered the best native wood for hubs of wheels. There is a great elm tree on Boston Common which is over two hundred years old, and another in Cambridge called the 'Washington Elm,' because near it or beneath its shade General Washington is said to have first drawn his sword on taking command of the American army. In 1744 the celebrated George Whitefield preached beneath this tree."

"I'm glad we have elm trees here," said Malcolm, "though I s'pose nobody ever did anything in particular under ours."

"You mean," replied his governess, laughing, "that they are not historical trees; but they are certainly very fine ones. There is another species of elm, the English, which is often seen in this country too. It is a very large and stately tree, but not so graceful as our own elm. It is distinguished from the American elm by its bark, which is darker and much more broken; by having one principal stem, which soars upward to a great height; and by its branches, which are thrown out more boldly and abruptly and at a larger angle. Its limbs stretch out horizontally or tend upward with an appearance of strength to the very extremity; in the American elm they are almost universally drooping at the end. Its leaves are closer, smaller, more numerous and of a darker color. In England this tree is a great favorite with those black and solemn birds the rooks. The poet Hood writes of it as

"'The tall, abounding elm that grows In hedgerows up and down, In field and forest, copse and park, And in the peopled town, With colonies of noisy rooks That nestle on its crown.'

"Some of these English elms are very ancient and of an immense size; one of them, known as the 'Chequer Elm,' measures thirty-one feet around the trunk, of which only the shell is left. It was planted seven hundred years ago. The Chipstead Elm is fifteen feet around; the Crawley Elm, thirty-five. A writer says, 'The ample branches of the Crawley Elm shelter Mayday gambols while troops of rustics celebrate the opening of green leaves and flowers. Yet not alone beneath its shade, but within the capacious hollow which time has wrought in the old tree, young children with their posies and weak and aged people find shelter during the rustic f 陟 es.'"

"Does that mean that people can sit inside the tree?" asked Clara. "I wish we had one to play house in where Hemlock Lodge is."

"That is one of the things, Clara," replied Miss Harson, "that people can have only in the place where they grow. In the South of England there is another great elm tree with a hollow trunk which has fitted into it a door fastened by a lock and key. A dozen people can be comfortably accommodated inside, and there is a story told of a woman and her infant who lived there for a time."

"What a funny house!" said Malcolm. "Just like a woodpecker's."

"Another great elm, near London, has a winding staircase cut within it, and a turret at the top where at least twenty persons can stand. One species of this tree, called the wych-, or witch-, elm, was believed by ignorant people to possess magical powers and to defend from the malice of witches the place on which it grew. Even now it is said that in remote parts of England the dairymaid flies to it as a resource on the days when she churns her butter. She gathers a twig from the tree and puts it into a little hole in the churn. If this practice were neglected, she confidently believes that she might go on churning all day without getting any butter."

"Isn't that silly?" exclaimed Clara.

"Very silly indeed," replied her governess; "but we must remember that the poor ignorant girl knows no better. The wood of the European elm is stronger than ours; it is hard and fine-grained, and brownish in color, and is much used in the building of ships, for hubs of wheels, axletrees and many other purposes. In France the leaves and shoots are used to feed cattle. In Russia the leaves of one variety are made into tea. The inner bark is in some places made into mats, and in Norway they kiln-dry it and grind it with corn as an ingredient in bread. So that the elm tree is almost as useful as it is beautiful."

CHAPTER IV.

MAJESTY AND STRENGTH: THE OAK.

"Here," said Miss Harson, "is a small branch from an oak tree containing the young leaves and the catkins, which come out together; for the oak belongs, like the willow and the maple, to the division of amentaceous plants."

"Oh dear!" sighed Clara at the hard name.

But Malcolm repeated:

"Amentaceous--ament. I know, Miss Harson: it's catkins"

"Yes, it means trees which produce their flowers in catkins, or looking as if strung on long drooping stems; and the oak is the monarch of this family, and in Great Britain of all the forest-trees. It is especially an English tree, although our woods contain several varieties. But they do not hold the pre-eminence in our forests that the oaks do in those of England. The oak ordinarily runs more to breadth than to height, and spreads itself out to a vast distance with an air of strength and grandeur. This is its striking character and what gives it its peculiar appearance. Oaks do not always go straight out, but crook and bend to right and left, upward and downward, abruptly or with a gentle sweep.

"The white oak is the handsomest species, and takes its name from the very light color of the bark on the trunk, by which it is easily known. The leaves are long in proportion to the width and deeply divided into lobes, of which there are three or four on each side. There is a great variety in the shape of oak-leaves, those of our white oak being long and slender, while the red oak has very broad ones, and the foliage of the scarlet oak is almost skeleton-like. The chestnut oak has leaves almost exactly like those of the chestnut. The acorns of the different varieties, too, differ in size and shape.

"There is so much to be said of the oak," continued Miss Harson, "it is such an ancient and venerable tree and has so many stories attached to it, that it is not easy to begin an account of it. The blossoms, perhaps, will be the best starting-point: and I should like to have you examine this branch and tell me if you see any difference in the blossoms."

"They are nearly all alike," said Malcolm, "but here at the ends of the twigs are one or two that look like buds."'

"That is just what I wanted you to notice," replied his governess, "for the flowers are of two kinds, one bearing the stamens, and the other the pistils. The flowers that bear the stamens grow on loose scaly catkins, as you may see in this branch. Those with the pistils are also in catkins, but very small, like a bud. The bud spreads into a little branchlet and bears the flowers at the tip. The calyx is not seen at first; it is a mere membrane covering the ovary. By degrees the ovary swells into the acorn and the membrane becomes part of the shell."

"I like acorns," said little Edith, "they're so nice to play with."

"But they're not nice to eat," said Clara.

"Some animals think they are," continued Miss Harson. "If you should come here in October, you would find the squirrels feasting on them. In old times in England the oaks were valued highly on account of their acorns, and great herds of swine were driven into the forests to feed upon them. In the time of the Saxons a crop of acorns often formed a part of the dowry bestowed upon the Saxon queens, and the king himself would be glad to accept a gift or grant of acorns; and the failure of the crop would be considered as a kind of famine. In those days laws were made to protect the oaks from being felled or injured, and a man who cut down a tree under the shadow of which thirty hogs could stand was fined three pounds. The herds of swine were placed under the care of a swineherd, whose sole employment was to keep them together, and they formed a staple part of the riches of the country. But when the Norman kings began to rule, they brought with them a passionate love of hunting and took possession of the forests as preserves for their favorite sport. The herds of swine were forbidden to roam about as heretofore, and their owners were reduced to poverty in consequence."

"Wasn't that wicked, Miss Harson?" asked Malcolm.

"Yes; it was both unjust and cruel, and it was one of the great grievances of the nation. Even at this day the laws for the protection of game are one of the grounds of ill-feeling on the part of the poor toward the nobles. In Spain the acorns have the taste of nuts, and are sold in the markets as an article of food. They grow abundantly in the woods and forests. Once, in time of war, a foreign army subsisted almost entirely on them. Herds of swine range the forests in Spain and feed luxuriously upon acorns, and the salted meats of Malaga, that are famous for their delicate flavor, are thought to owe it to this cause. Some of our American Indians depend upon acorns and fish for their winter food; and when the acorns drop from the tree, they are buried in sand and soaked in water to draw out the bitter taste."

"I shouldn't like them," said Clara, with a wry face at the thought of such food.

"Well, dear," replied her governess, laughing, "as you are not an Indian, you will probably not be called upon to like them; but it would be better to eat acorns than to starve. You may have noticed the trunk and branches of the oak are often gnarled and knotted, and this helps to give the tree its appearance of great strength. It is just as strong as it looks, and for building-purposes it lasts longer than any other wood. Beams and rafters of oak are found in old English houses, showing among the brick-work, and many of these half-timbered houses, as they are called, were built hundreds of years ago.

"Bedsteads and other articles of furniture, too, were 'built' in those days, rather than made, for they were not expected to be moved about; and a heavy oak bedstead is still in existence which is said to have belonged to King Richard III. It is curiously carved, and the king rested upon it the night before the battle of Bosworth Field, where he was killed. Clumsy as the bedstead was, he took it about with him from place to place; but after the fatal battle it passed into the hands of various owners, and nothing remarkable was discovered about it until the king had been dead a hundred years. By that time the bedstead had come into the possession of a woman who found a fortune in it. One morning, says the story, as she was making the bed, she heard a chinking sound, and saw, to her great delight, a piece of money drop on the floor. Of course she at once set about examining the bedstead, and found that the lower part of it was hollow and contained a treasure. Three hundred pounds--a fortune in those days--was brought to light, having remained hidden all those years. As King Richard was not there to claim his gold, the woman quickly possessed herself of it. But, as it happened, she had better have remained in ignorance and poverty. As soon as the matter became known one of her servants robbed her of the gold, and even caused her death. Thus it was said in the neighborhood that 'King Richard's gold' did nobody any good."

The children were very much pleased with this story, and Malcolm said that he always liked to hear about people who found gold and things.

"I think that I do, myself," replied Miss Harson, "although, as in this poor woman's case and in many others, gold is not the best thing to find. It often brings with it so much sorrow and sin as to be a curse to its owner. The only safe treasure is that laid up in heaven, where 'neither moth nor rust doth corrupt, and where thieves do not break through nor steal,'

"From the very earliest times the oak has been used for shipbuilding. The Saxons, we are told, kept a formidable fleet of vessels with curved bottoms and the prow and poop adorned with representations of the head and tail of some grotesque and fabulous creature. King Alfred had many vessels that carried sixty oars and were entirely of oak. A vessel supposed to be of his time has been discovered in the bed of a river in Kent, and after the lapse of so many centuries it is as sound as ever and as hard as iron."

"Do oak trees ever have apples on 'em?" asked Clara. "In a story that I read there was something about 'oak-apples.'"

"They are not apples such as we eat, or fruit in any sense," said her governess. "They are the work of a species of fly called Cynips, which is very apt to attack the oak. 'The female insect is armed with a sharp weapon called an ovipositor, which she plunges into a leaf and makes a wound. Here she lays her eggs; and when she has done so, she flies away and we hear no more of her. But the wound she has made disturbs the circulation of the sap. It flows round and round the eggs as though it had met with some foreign body it would fain remove. Very soon the eggs are in the midst of a ball-like and fleshy chamber--the most suitable provision for them, and one which the parent-insect had provided by means of puncturing the leaf. As the eggs are hatched the grubs will find themselves safely housed and in the midst of an abundance of food.'"

"Well," exclaimed Malcolm, in great disgust, "apple is a queer name for a ball full of little flies!"

"It's a very pretty ball, though," said Miss Harson, "with a smooth skin and tinged with red or yellow, like a ripe apple. If it is cut open, a number of granules are seen, each containing a grub embedded in a fruit-like substance. The grub undergoes its transformation, and in due course emerges a perfect insect. These pretty pink-and-white apples used to be gathered by English boys on the twenty-ninth of May, which was called 'Oak-Apple Day.'"

"Did they eat 'em?" asked Edith.

"I do not see how they could, dear," was the reply; "they were probably gathered just to look at. Yet 'May-apples,' which grow, you will remember, on the wild azalea and the swamp honeysuckle, are often eaten, and they are formed in the same way; so we will not be too positive about the oak-apples."

"What are oak-galls, Miss Harson?" asked Malcolm. "Are they the same as oak-apples?"

"Not quite the same," was the reply, although both are produced by the same insect. This is what one of our English books says of them: 'When the acorn itself is wounded, it becomes a kind of monstrosity, and remains on the stalk like an irregularly-shaped ball. It is called a "nut-gall," and is found principally on a small oak, a native of the southern and central parts of Europe. All these oak-apples and nut-galls are of importance, but the latter more especially, and they form an important article of commerce. A substance called "gallic acid" resides in the oak; and when the puncture is made by the cynips, it flows in great abundance to the wound. Gallic acid is one of the ingredients used in dyeing stuffs and cloths, and therefore the supply yielded by the nut-gall is highly welcome. The nut-galls are carefully collected from the small oak on which they are found, the Pyreneean oak. It is easily known by the dense covering of down on the young leaves, that appear some weeks later than the leaves of the common oak. The galls are pounded and boiled, and into the infusion thus made the stuffs about to be dyed are dipped,'"

"I should think," said Clara, "that people would plant oak trees everywhere, when they are so useful. Is anything done with the bark?"

"Yes," said her governess; "the bark, which is very rough, is valuable for tanning leather and for medicine. The element which has the effect of turning raw hide or skin into leather is called tannin; it is also found in the bark of some other trees and in tropical plants."

"Didn't people use to worship oak trees," asked Malcolm--"people who lived ever so long ago?"

"You are thinking of the Druids, who lived in old times in Britain and Gaul," replied Miss Harson, "and whose strange heathen rites were practiced in oak-groves; and they really did consider the tree sacred. These Druids have left their traces in some parts of England and France in rows of huge stones set upright; and wherever an immense stone was found lying on two others, in the shape of a table, there had been a Druid altar, where the priest offered sacrifices, often of human beings. So horrible may be a so-called religion that men themselves devise, and that has not come from the true God.

"It was an article in the Druids' creed, and one to which they strictly adhered, that no temple with a covered roof was to be built in honor of the gods. All the places appointed for public worship were in the open air, and generally on some eminence from which the moon and stars might be observed; for to the heavenly bodies much adoration was offered. But to afford shelter from wind or rain, and also to ensure privacy and shut out all external objects, the place fixed upon, either for teaching their disciples or for carrying out the rites of their idolatrous worship, was in the recess of some grove or wood. An oak-grove was supposed to be the favorite of the gods whom they ignorantly worshiped, and therefore the Druids declared the oak to be a sacred tree. The Druid priest always bound a wreath of oak-leaves on his forehead before he would perform any religious ceremony. One of these ceremonies was to go in search of the mistletoe, which sometimes grows on the oak and was considered as sacred as the tree itself, being much used in their worship. One priest would climb to the branch on which the misletoe was growing and cut it with a golden knife, while another priest stood below and held out his white robe to receive it.

"These sacred groves were all cut down by the Romans, who waged fierce war against the Druids, and nothing is left of them now but the circles of stones that formed their temples. At a place called Stonehenge, 'cromlechs,' or altar-tables, are still standing, and very ancient oaks stood in a circle round these stones for many centuries after the Druids were swept away."

"Miss Harson," said Clara when all had expressed their horror of the Druids and rejoiced that they were swept away, "are there any oak trees in the Bible?"

"Look and see," was the reply; "and first you may find Genesis xxxv. 4."

Clara read:

"'And they gave unto Jacob all the strange gods which were in their hands, and all their earrings which were in their ears; and Jacob hid them under the oak which was by Shechem.'"

"In the eighth verse of the same chapter," said Miss Harson, "we read that Rebekah's nurse was buried under an oak at Bethel. We are told in the book of Joshua[2] that 'Joshua took a great stone and set it up there under an oak, that was by the sanctuary of the Lord;' and in Judges[3], 'There came an angel of the Lord and sat under an oak which was in Ophrah.'--Malcolm, you may read Second Samuel, eighteenth chapter, ninth verse."

[2] Josh. xxiv. 26.

[3] Judg. vi. II.

Malcolm read:

"'And Absalom met the servants of David. And Absalom rode upon a mule, and the mule went under the thick boughs of a great oak, and his head caught hold of the oak, and he was taken up between the heaven and the earth; and the mule that was under him went away.'"

"Poor Absalom!" said Edith, softly. "Wasn't that dreadful?"

"Yes, dear," replied her governess, "it was dreadful; but it is still more dreadful that Absalom was such a wicked man. In Isaiah[4] we read of the oaks of Bashan, that, like the cedars of Lebanon, were 'high and lifted up,' and the oaks of Bashan are mentioned again in Zechariah[5]. Several varieties of the oak are found in Palestine.

[4] Isa. ii. 13.

[5] Zech. xi. 2.

[Illustration: ABRAHAM'S OAK, NEAR HEBRON.]

"In his Ride Through Palestine, Dr. Dulles tells of a great oak near Hebron known as 'Abraham's oak,' supposed to occupy the ground where the patriarch pitched his tent under the oaks of Mamre. It is an aged tree, and a grand one. Here is a picture of it, from the Ride[6]. The crests and sides of the hills beyond the Jordan are still clothed, as in ancient times, with magnificent oaks.

[6] See page 85

"We get a good idea of the strength and durability of this wood from the fact that there is an old wooden church near Ongar, in Essex, the nave of which is composed of half logs of oak roughly fastened by wooden pegs. The ancient fabric dates back to the time of King Edmund, who was slain by the robber Leolf in the year A.D. 946. The oaken church was hurriedly put together--according to report--in order to make a temporary receptacle for the body of the murdered prince on its way to burial. Be that as it may, it was afterward used as a parish church, and, though the oaken logs are corroded by the weather, they are still sound, and, having been beaten by the storms of a thousand winters, bid fair to defy those of a thousand more."

"I should think, then," said Malcolm, "that people would always build their houses with oak if it lasts so long."

"Yet they do not do this even in England," was the reply, "where the trees grow to such an immense size and the ancient buildings still in existence prove the great endurance of the oak. Now brick and stone and iron are used, which outlast any wood. And now," continued Miss Harson, "I am going to tell you something about a foreign species of this tree which I am sure will surprise you. It is found in the South of Europe and in Algeria, and is called the cork oak."

"'The cork oak'!" exclaimed Clara, quite as much surprised as she was expected to be. "Do the corks that come in bottles grow on it?"

"Not just in that shape, dear, but they are made from its bark. The outside bark, or epidermis, consists of a thin, transparent, tissue-like substance, which covers not only the bark, but the whole of the tree, stem, leaves and branches, and beneath the epidermis is found a layer of cellular tissue, generally green. It covers the trunk and branches, fills up the spaces between the veins of the leaves and contains the sap, which flows in canals arranged for it in the most beautiful and wonderful manner. In one species of oak this layer--which is called the suber--assumes a peculiar character and is of remarkable thickness. When the tree is some five years old, its whole energy is directed toward the increase of the suber. A mass of cells is formed with great rapidity, and layer upon layer is added, until that part of the trunk grows so unwieldy that it would crack and split of its own accord. But such a thing is rarely allowed to happen: the suber is of too much value to man. After it is taken from the tree and has undergone due preparation, it appears in our shops and houses under the name of cork"

"I should like to see how they get it," said Malcolm.

"The trunk is regularly marked around in deep cuts, which begin close to the branches and go down almost to the roots. A ladder is used to mount to the upper part of the trunk, and the cuts, or incisions, are made with a long knife or with an axe. Then they strip off the sheets of cork between the circles. This operation is a very delicate one, and requires much care and skill lest the inner part should be injured. If the operation is carried out successfully, the cork-like substance will grow again and become as abundant as ever.

"The next thing to be done to the pieces of bark is partially to burn, or char, them, and also to make them quite flat, as they come from the trunk in a rounded shape. The burning makes the pores close up, so that the liquid in a vessel for which it is used as a stopper cannot come through; and this is done over a brisk fire, in what is called a burning-yard. Another process, called rounding, removes every trace of the fire, unless the cork has been too much burned, and then, having already been flattened by the pressure of heavy stones, it is ready for the cork-maker, who cuts the material first into strips and then into squares according to the size of corks wanted.

"Cork is very light and elastic, and can be used successfully in contrivances for the rescue of men from the perils of the deep. The cork jacket and the lifeboat have been the means of saving many lives, for cork will float on the surface of the water and bear up the person wearing the jacket and the shipwrecked people in the lifeboat. 'The shallowness of the boat and the bulk of cork within allow but little room for water; so that even when filled it is in no danger of overturning or sinking, like other crafts. Also, the lifeboat can move across the waves with perfect safety, and can make its way from one object to another in a broken sea as easily as an ordinary boat can pass from one ship to another.'"

The children declared that the cork-oak was the best tree of all, but they agreed with their governess that the entire oak family was made up of grand and useful trees.

"Our American oaks," said Miss Harson, "are very handsome in autumn because of their brilliant foliage; the scarlet oak, which turns to a deep crimson and keeps its leaves longer than any of the other forest trees, is the most showy of the species. But we have no cork oaks, and no oaks that we know to be a thousand years old. There was once a famous oak in this country, called the 'Charter Oak,' which fell to the ground in August, 1856, before any of us were born. I wonder if you would like to hear the story about it?"

This question was thought extremely funny by three such devourers of stories as the little Kyles, and they eagerly assured their governess that they would like it.

"If that is really the case," continued Miss Harson, smiling at the excited faces, "I must tell you the history of

"THE CHARTER OAK.

"This tree grew in Hartford, Connecticut, and it is said that before the English governor Wyllis went there to live his steward, whom he had sent on before to get a house ready for him, came near cutting down this very oak. He was clearing away the trees around it on the hillside when a party of Indians appeared and begged him to leave that particular tree, because, they said, 'it had been the guide of their ancestors for centuries.' So the oak was spared; even then it was old and hollow.

"King Charles II. granted the people of Connecticut a very liberal charter of rights, which was publicly read in the Assembly at Hartford and declared to belong for ever to them and their successors. A committee was appointed to take charge of it, under a solemn oath that they would preserve this palladium of the rights of the people.

"When James II., the tyrannical brother of Charles II., came to the throne, he changed the government of New England and ordered the people of Connecticut to give up their charter. This they refused to do; and when a third command from the king had been sent to them, they called a special meeting of the Assembly, under their own governor, Treat, and resolved to hold on to the charter which had been given them.

"On the 31st of October, 1687, Sir Edmund Andros, attended by members of his council and a bodyguard of sixty soldiers, entered Hartford to take the charter by force. The General Assembly was in session; he was received with courtesy, but with coldness. He entered the assembly-room and publicly demanded the charter. Remonstrances were made, and the session was protracted till evening. The governor and his associates appeared to yield. The charter was brought in and laid upon the table. Sir Edmund thought that he had succeeded, when suddenly the lights were all put out, and total darkness followed. There was no noise, no conflict, but all was quiet. When the candles were again lighted, the charter was gone! Sir Edmund was disconcerted. He declared the government of Connecticut to be in his own hands, and that the colony was annexed to Massachusetts and the other New England colonies, and proceeded to appoint officers. Captain Jeremiah Wadsworth, a patriot of those times, had hidden the charter in the hollow of Wyllis's oak, whence it was afterward known as the Charter Oak."

"Then the English governor couldn't get it!" exclaimed Malcolm, delightedly. "Wasn't that splendid?"

"It was a grand hiding-place, certainly, for no one would think of looking inside a tree for such a thing as that, and they were grand men who preserved their country's liberties in those trying times. But more peaceful years were at hand. About eighteen months after the charter had disappeared so mysteriously, the tyrant James II. was compelled to give up his throne to his daughter and son-in-law, the prince and princess of Orange, and Governor Treat and his associates again took the government of Connecticut under the old charter, which the hollow oak had faithfully kept from harm. No tree in our whole country has received more attention than this historic Hartford oak; and when, at last, its mere shell of a trunk was laid low by a storm, it seemed as if a large part of the city had been swept away.

"Ancient oaks are apt to be almost entirely without branches; the huge trunk, with an opening at the top, and often with one also at the bottom, stands like a maimed giant, just tottering, perhaps, to its fall, because of the decay going on within, while outside all seems fair and sound. It was so with the Charter Oak; and when this monarch of the forest was unexpectedly laid low, rich and poor, great and small, were gathered to mourn its loss. A dirge was played and all the bells in the city were tolled at sundown, for this monument of the past was a link gone that could not be replaced."

"Thank you, Miss Harson," said Clara; "true stories are so nice! But I wish I had seen the Charter Oak before it was blown down."

"You could not have done that, dear," was the reply, "unless you had been born about thirty years sooner."

CHAPTER V.

BEAUTY AND GRACE: THE ASH.

"What tree comes next, Miss Harson?" asked Clara, on an April day that was mild enough for the piazza. "You told us so many interesting things about the oak that I suppose we needn't expect to hear of another tree like that."

"No," was the reply; "not just like that, perhaps, for the oak is grand and venerable above all our familiar trees, but the ash, which is more especially an American tree, belongs to a large and interesting family, and I am quite sure that you will very much like to hear something about it. I have put it next to the oak because there is a sort of rivalry between the two as to which can get on its spring dress the soonest, and an old English rhyme says,

"'If the oak's before the ash, Then you may expect a splash; But if the ash is 'fore the oak, Then you must beware a soak.'"

"That must mean," said Malcolm, after considering this rather puzzling verse, "that it'll rain any way."

"I think it does," replied Miss Harson, with a smile at Malcolm's air of deep thought, "and it is quite safe to say that in England. But, as 'a soak' sounds more serious than 'a splash,' it is to be hoped that the ash will not get ahead of the oak. I do not know what they are doing in England this year, but here the oak is a day or two ahead. The foliage of the ash is entirely different, as it has pinnate leaves, which means leaves arranged in two rows, one on each side of a common stem, or petiole, like--What, Clara?"

"Rose-leaves," was the prompt reply.

"And leaves of the locust trees on the other side of the road," added Malcolm.

"And the sumac," said their governess, "and a number of others that might be mentioned. This kind of foliage is always graceful, and the ash is one of our largest and handsomest trees. It is said to be more common in America than in any other part of the globe. In Europe, because of its beauty, it is called the painter's tree. It is a particularly neat and regular-looking tree, and its smooth gray trunk is higher than that of most trees before any branches appear. Where is there a tree on the grounds answering this description, Malcolm?"

"Down at the end of the vegetable-garden," was the reply, "and close beside the laundry."

"Yes; you are really learning to distinguish trees very well. There are several species--the white, red, black and mountain ash. The white ash is a graceful tree, rising in the forest to the height of seventy or eighty feet, with a straight trunk and a diameter of three feet or more at the base. On an open plain it throws out its branches, with a gentle double curvature, to a distance on every side, and forms a broad, round head of great beauty. The flowers of the ash are greenish white in color and appear with the leaves in loose clusters. 'The trunk of our largest American ash is covered with a whitish bark which in very young trees is nearly smooth; on older trees it is broken by deep furrows into irregular plates, and on very old stems it becomes smooth again, from the rough plates scaling off. The branches are grayish green dotted with gray or white.' Now who can tell me something about this tree?"

"I know that furniture is made of the wood," said Clara, "because that pretty set in the large spare-room is ash. And it is very light-colored."

"The wood is used for a great many things," replied Miss Harson, "and the ash has been called the husbandman's tree because the timber is so much in demand for farming-implements, and for articles that need to be both strong and light. It does not last so long as the oak, but it is more elastic and can better resist sudden shocks and jerks; it is therefore particularly desirable for the spokes of wheels and ladders and the beams of floors. Staircases were made of it in olden times, and they may still be found in some English halls and abbeys. The forest ash makes better oars than any other wood, and the tree has so many good qualities that an old English poet spoke of it as

"'The ash for nothing ill.'

"But Malcolm looks as if he had something to say, and I shall be very happy to hear it."

"It is only about the red berries that they bear in autumn, Miss Harson; it looks queer to see berries growing on a tree."

"The mountain ash is the only one that has berries," replied his governess, "and the bloom is in clusters of white flowers. The berries are sometimes dark red and often of a bright scarlet, and they remain on the tree during the winter, to the great delight of the birds. We should find them very sour, although pretty to look at; but the little feathered wanderers eat them with great relish when the snows of winter make bird-food scarce and the bright-red berries gleam out most invitingly. In some parts of Europe the berries are dried and ground into flour. The rowan, or roan, tree is the English name of the mountain ash, and in some parts of Great Britain it is called witchen, because of its supposed power against witches and evil spirits and all their spells. In old times branches of it were hung about houses and stables and cow-sheds, for it was thought that

"'witches have no power Where there is roan-tree wood.'"

"But that isn't true, is it?" asked Edith.

"No, dear, not true of either the witches or the wood. But ignorant people believe a great many foolish things, and the leaves and twigs of the ash tree were thought to have peculiar virtue. In some places it was once the practice to pluck an ash-leaf in every case where the leaflets were of even number, and to say,

"'Even ash, I do thee pluck, Hoping thus to meet good luck; If no luck I get from thee, Better far be on the tree.'"

"It sounds like what children say on finding a four-leafed clover," said Clara.

"It is on the same principle," was the reply, "for clover-leaves grow naturally in threes and ash-leaves in sevens. Both rhymes are equally silly where luck is concerned, and those who believe God's words--that even 'the hairs of our head are all numbered'--will have no faith in 'luck.' In old times the ash was believed to perform wonderful cures of various kinds, and in remote parts of England a little mouse called the shrew-mouse bore a very bad character. If a horse or cow had pains in its limbs, they were said to be caused by a shrew-mouse running over it. Our forefathers provided themselves with what they called a shrew-ash, in order to meet the case. The shrew-ash was nothing more than an ash tree in the trunk of which a hole had been bored and a poor little shrew-mouse put in, with many charms and incantations happily long since forgotten."

"And couldn't the poor little mouse get out again?" asked Edith.

"I am afraid not, dear; and we can only rejoice that we did not live in those dark days. Among other beliefs in its virtues, the leaves and wood of the ash were regarded throughout Northern Europe as a protection from all manner of snakes, and in harvest-time children were suspended in their cradles from the branches of tall ash trees while their mothers were working in the harvest-field below. Even now serpents are said to dislike the tree so much that they will not come near it, and the leaf is considered a cure for the bite of a poisonous snake. I have been told that an ash-leaf rubbed on a mosquito-bite will at once take out the sting and itching, and no better remedy can be found for the sting of a bee or a wasp."

"It's ever so much nicer than mud," said Clara, who had rather a talent for getting into hornets' nests.

"But the mud, you see, is always to be had," replied Miss Harson, "while ash-leaves do not grow everywhere; and I do not know that they have any power to cure the sting.

"The other species of ash found in this country are not so important as the white, but the black ash is remarkable as the slenderest deciduous tree of its height to be found in the forest. It is often seventy or eighty feet tall, with a trunk not more than a foot around. The color of the trunk is a dark granite-gray and the bark is rough. The wood is remarkable for its toughness, and for making baskets the Indians prefer it to any other, except the trunk of a young white oak.

"The red ash is very much like the white, but the wood is less valuable. It is a spreading, broad-headed tree, and the trunk is erect and branching. It is not so tall as the black ash, yet its trunk is three times as thick.

"A species of ash grows in Sicily that yields a substance called manna which used to be valuable as a medicine, and this manna is obtained in the same way as maple-sap--by making holes or incisions in the bark of the tree. At the proper season the persons whose business it is to collect manna begin to make incisions, one after the other, up the stem. The manna flows out like clear water, but it soon congeals and becomes a solid substance. It has a sweet taste, and while in a liquid state runs into a leaf of the tree that has been inserted in the wound. Afterward it flows into a vessel placed below, from which it is carried away and shipped off to other countries."

"Is there any story about the ash?" asked Malcolm.

"Not much of a story, dear," was the reply--"only a little legend of the manna trees; but, such as it is, you shall have it:

"The king of Naples, it is said, fenced a number of trees round and forbade any to collect the store they yielded unless they paid a tribute. By this means the royal revenue would be largely increased. But, according to the story, the manna trees, as if they disapproved of this ungenerous arrangement, refused to yield any manna, and suddenly became bare and barren. Upon this the king, finding his scheme a failure, revoked the tax and took away the fence. Then the trees poured out their manna, as usual, in the greatest abundance; so that it was said, 'When the king found he could not make a gain of what Providence had freely bestowed, he gave up the attempt and left the manna as free as God had given it.'

"There, now!" said Miss Harson; "after this long talk, you had better run off and see if there is not a tree somewhere on the grounds, with two ropes attached to it, that will bear better fruit than any tree we have studied yet."

The trio laughed and raced for the swing, which was first reached by Clara, who seated herself all ready for the push which Malcolm would not grudge, for he pronounced his sister sweeter than apple or peach; and so she was.

CHAPTER VI.

THE OLIVE TREE.

"The ash," said Miss Harson, "has some relations of which, I think, you will be rather surprised to hear. These relations are both trees and shrubs, and the lilac, for instance, is one of them."

"Why, they don't look a bit alike," exclaimed Clara.

"No, they certainly do not; for, although this fragrant shrub often grows as large as a tree, it is quite different from the ash tree. Yet both belong to the olive family."

"The kind of olives that papa likes to eat at dinner, and that you and I don't like, Miss Harson?" asked Malcolm.

"The very same," replied his governess; "only that we are speaking now of the tree on which the olives grow. It is well said that the very name of 'olive' suggests the idea of Palestine and the sunny lands of the East. The olive tree is one of the most prominent trees of the Bible. It is mentioned in the very earliest part of the Scriptures, in the book of Genesis. I wonder if some one can tell me about it?"

"I remember: a dove found a leaf when it was raining and brought it to Noah in the ark," said little Edith, quickly.

"The rain had stopped falling, dear, after the deluge, and the waters were receding, or falling, when Noah sent forth the dove a second time to see what it would find. Here is the verse: 'And the dove came in to him in the evening; and lo, in her mouth was an olive leaf pluckt off; so Noah knew that the waters were abated from off the earth[7].' For this reason the olive-branch is a common emblem of peace. The olive tree is often mentioned in other parts of the Bible, and was considered one of the most valuable trees of Palestine, which is described as 'a land of oil-olive and honey.' It is not nearly so handsome as some other trees of the Holy Land, nor is it grand-looking or graceful. The leaves, which are long for the width, and smooth, are dark green on the upper side and silvery beneath; they generally grow in pairs. The fruit is shaped like a plum; it is green when first formed, then paler in color; and when quite ripe, it is black."

[7] Gen. viii. 9.

"But those that papa eats are olive-color," said Clara.

"Yes," replied Miss Harson, smiling, "but all these hues I have mentioned are olive-color in some stage of the fruit; and it is in the green stage, before it is quite ripe, that it is gathered for preserving."

"But that isn't preserves, is it?" asked Malcolm, drawing up his mouth at the recollection of an olive he had once tried to eat. "I thought preserves were always sweet."

"That is the shape in which you are accustomed to them, Malcolm; but to preserve a thing means to keep it from decay, and salt and vinegar will do this as well as sugar. Preserves of this kind are what you call 'puckery.'--As to the color, Clara, 'olive-green' is a color by itself, because of its peculiar tint. It is a gray green instead of a blue or yellow green, and it has a very dull effect. The fruit is produced only once in two years, and in bearing-season the tree is loaded with white blossoms that drop to the ground like flakes of snow. It is said that not one in a hundred of these numerous flowers becomes an olive. Here," continued Miss Harson, pointing to a page of a book in her hand, "is a representation of an olive-branch with some of the plum-shaped fruit. The branch, you see, is hard and stiff-looking."

"I should think the tree would be prettier when all those white flowers are on it," said little Edith.

"It is--much prettier," replied her governess--"but not so useful. The fruit of the olive is so valuable that numbers of people depend upon it for their support. The wood, too, is very hard and durable, and, as it takes a fine polish, it is used for making many ornamental articles."

"And where does the olive-oil come from?" asked Clara. "Do they make holes in the tree for it, as they do for maple-sap?"

Malcolm was about to exclaim at this idea, but he remembered just in time that, should Miss Harson happen to question him, he himself could not tell where the oil came from.

"The oil is pressed from the olives," was the reply; "a large, vigorous tree is said to yield a thousand pounds of it. It is such an important article of commerce in the regions where it is prepared that every one desires to get as much as he can out of his olive trees, but those who are too greedy of gain will spoil the quality of the oil to make a larger quantity. The small olive of Syria is considered the most delicate, and Italian olives also are very fine; those of Spain are larger and coarser. The best olive-oil comes from the south-eastern portion of France and is a clear, pure liquid; it is obtained from the first pressing of the fruit. This must be only a gentle squeeze, to get the purest oil: the quality usually sold is made by a heavier pressure; and then, when the olives are worked over again, come the dregs, which are not fit for table-use."

"Do they mash 'em, like making apples into cider?" asked Malcolm.

"Something like that; and the olive-farmers take the most anxious care of their orchards, for they know that the more olives the more oil. This with the Italians means a living, and one of their proverbs says, 'If you wish to leave a competency to your grandchildren, plant an olive.' The poorest of the fruit is eaten in their own families, 'to save it,' and, as it does not taste so well, it will go much farther. They do not eat olives, though, as we see them eaten--one or two as a relish; but a respectable dishful is provided for each person, instead of the bread and potatoes which they do not have."

"I'd rather have the bread and potatoes," said Clara, "and I'm glad that I don't have to eat a whole plate of olives."

"If you had always been accustomed to having olives, as the Italians are," replied Miss Harson, "you would think them very nice. I do not suppose that their children ever think how much more inviting are the olives that are kept for sale. Olives intended for exportation are gathered while still green, usually in the month of October. They are soaked for some hours in the strongest lye, to get rid of their bitterness, and are afterward allowed to stand for a fortnight in frequently-changed fresh water, in order to be perfectly purified of the lye. It only then remains to preserve them in common salt and water, when they are ready for export."

"That's what they taste of," exclaimed Malcolm--"salt; and I don't like salt things."

"I think," said his governess, with a smile, "that I have seen a boy whom I know enjoying sliced ham and tongue very much indeed."

"So I do, Miss Harson," was the eager reply; "but ham and tongue, you know, don't taste like olives."

"No, because they are ham and tongue. But they certainly taste salty, and that is what you object to. It is generally found that sweeping assertions are not very safe ones. But to come back to our olive tree: it is an evergreen, and it grows very easily. The readiness with which a twig will take root reminds us of the willow. A fine grove of olive trees at Messa, in Morocco, was accidentally planted. It is said that one of the kings of the dynasty of Saddia, being on a military expedition, encamped here with his army. The pegs with which the cavalry picketed their horses were cut from olive trees in the neighborhood, and, some sudden cause of alarm leading to the abandonment of the position, the pegs were left in the ground. Making the best of the situation, the pegs developed into the handsomest group of olive trees in the district."

The children wondered if any trees had ever been planted in such a strange way before, and little Edith said thoughtfully,

"But, Miss Harson, why don't good people go around and plant trees wherever there aren't any? It would be so nice!"

"Some good people do plant trees, dear, wherever they can," replied her governess, "thinking, as they say, of those who are to come after them; a great many roadside trees have grown in this way. But no one is allowed to meddle with other people's property; waste-places might easily be beautified with trees if the owners cared for anything but for their own present interests. But here is something you will like to hear about the olives of Palestine: 'They are all planted together in the grove like the trees in a forest, and it would seem scarcely possible for the owners to distinguish their own property. But when the fruit is getting ripe, watchmen are appointed to guard the grove and prevent a single olive from being touched even by the person who has a right to the tree.'--You do not look as if you would like that, Malcolm."

"Indeed I wouldn't!" replied the boy. "I rather think I'd take my own olives whenever I wanted 'em."

"Not if you lived where all were agreed on this point, as they seem to be in Palestine.--'Days pass on, and the autumn is at hand before the governor of the district issues the wished-for proclamation; then the watchmen are removed. Immediately the scene becomes a most animated one. The grove is alive with an eager throng of men, women and children shaking down the precious fruit. It is, however, scarcely possible to bring every berry down, nor would it seem desirable, since after this great harvest comes the gleaning-time, when the poor, who have no olive trees, are permitted to come into the grove and shake down what is left.'"

"Isn't there something about that in the Bible, Miss Harson?" asked Clara.

"Yes; it is in the book of the prophet Isaiah, 'Yet gleaning grapes shall be left in it, as the shaking of an olive tree, two or three berries in the top of the uppermost bough, four or five in the outmost fruitful branches thereof, saith the Lord God of Israel[8].' This is a prophecy about God's people, but the Jews were told by God to leave something, when they were harvesting, for the poor to glean. Does it not seem wonderful that the mighty Ruler of the universe should condescend to such small things? But nothing is small with him, and we see that his loving care extends to the poorest and the meanest."

[8] Isa. xvii. 6.

"Miss Harson," asked Edith, with great earnestness, "has each of our hairs got a number on it? I couldn't find any."

The young lady could scarcely keep from smiling, but she was obliged to call Malcolm to order, and even Clara seemed amused at her little sister's queer interpretation of the loving words, "The very hairs of your head are all numbered."

Miss Harson took her youngest pupil on her knee and explained to her the meaning of our Saviour's words in Luke xii. 7, where it is added, "Fear not,", because the heavenly Father's loving care is always around us.

"It was a natural mistake," she continued, "for a very little girl to make; but we must not try to find amusement in mistakes about God's word. Many grown people are irreverent in this way without knowing it: perhaps they were not properly taught when they were children. But my children must not have this excuse, and I want them all to promise me that they will never utter nor listen to words from the Bible in any other but a reverent manner."

All promised, Malcolm with a flushed face and subdued tone; and Edith felt that one of the great puzzles of her small existence had been solved.

"Oil is the most important product of the olive tree," said Miss Harson, "and it has well been called its richness and fatness. The great demand for it in Europe and Asia prevents the best quality from being sent abroad, and it is said that even the most wealthy foreigners seldom get it pure. It is a most important article of food, taking the place held by butter and lard with us. Innumerable lamps, too, are kept burning by means of this oil, and so varied are its uses in the East that it was a greater thing than we can understand for the prophet Habakkuk to say, 'Although the labor of the olive shall fail, ... yet will I rejoice in the Lord, I will joy in the God of my salvation.' Job says, 'The rock poured me out rivers of oil[9];' this means the oil of the olive, which will thrive on the sides and tops of rocky hills where there is scarcely any earth. It is a very long-lived tree, as well as an evergreen; the Psalmist says, 'I am like a green olive tree in the house of God.'"

[9] Job xxiii. 6.

"What does a wild olive tree mean, Miss Harson?" asked Clara.

"It means, dear, one that has grown without being cultivated, like our wild cherry and plum trees. The wild olive is smaller than the other, and inferior to it in every way. There are a great many olive trees in Palestine, and a place where they must have been very plentiful is called by a name which we often see in the Bible.--What is it, Malcolm?"

"Is it 'the Mount of Olives'?" said Malcolm.

"Yes, and it is sometimes called 'Olivet.' It is mentioned in the Old Testament as well as in the New. In Second Samuel it is written: 'And David went up by the ascent of Mount Olivet, and wept as he went up, and had his head covered, and he went barefoot: and all the people that was with him covered every man his head, and they went up, weeping as they went up[10].'"

[10] 2 Sam. xv. 30.

"What was the matter?" asked Edith.

"King David's wicked son Absalom had risen up against his father because he wished to be king in his stead. You remember how he was caught by the head in the boughs of an oak during the very battle that he was fighting for this purpose; so we know that he did not succeed in his wicked plan, but lost his life instead.--The Mount of Olives is described as 'a ridge running north and south on the east side of Jerusalem, its summit about half a mile from the city wall and separated from it by the valley of the Kidron. It is composed of a chalky limestone, the rocks everywhere showing themselves. The olive trees that formerly covered it and gave it its name are now represented by a few trees and clumps of trees. There are three prominent summits on the ridge; of these, the southernmost, which is lower than the other two, is now known as 'the Mount of Offence,' originally 'the Mount of Corruption,' because Solomon defiled it with idolatrous worship. Over this ridge passes the road to Bethany, the most frequented route to Jericho and the Jordan. The side of the Mount of Olives toward the west contains many tombs cut in the rock. The central summit rises two hundred feet above Jerusalem and presents a fine view of the city, and, indeed, of the whole region, including the mountains of Ephraim on the north, the valley of the Jordan on the east, a part of the Dead Sea on the south-east, and beyond it Kerak, in the mountains of Moab. Perhaps no spot on earth unites so fine a view with so many memorials of the most solemn and important events. Over this hill the Saviour often climbed in his journeys to and from the Holy City. Gethsemane lay at its foot on the west, and Bethany on its eastern slope.'"

During the reading of this description of the Mount of Olives, Miss Harson showed the children pictures of the different spots mentioned, and thus they were not likely soon to forget what had been told them.

"Who can repeat some words from the New Testament about this mountain?" asked Miss Harson.

"'Jesus went unto the Mount of Olives,'" said Clara, who had learned this verse in her Sunday lesson, "and it is the first verse of the eighth chapter of St. John."

"And the verse just before it, at the end of the seventh chapter," replied her governess, "says that 'every man went unto his own house,' but 'Jesus went unto the Mount of Olives.' In another place it is said that 'at night he went out and abode in the Mount of Olives,' and in still another that he 'continued all night in prayer to God,' probably on the same mountain."

"And can people really go and see the very same Mount of Olives now?" asked Malcolm, eagerly.

"The very same," was the reply, "except, as I just read to you, many of the olive trees that gave it its name are no longer there. The Garden of Gethsemane, too, the most sacred spot near the mountain, is much changed, and a traveler who saw it lately says:

"'At the foot of the Mount of Olives is a garden enclosed by a wall. There are paths and there are plots of flowers, the work of loving hands in recent years. The flowers speak of to-day, but there are olive trees in the garden that testify of the history of far-away years. Their venerable trunks, gnarled and rugged, are like the rough, marred binding of old books, shutting in a history going back to a far-off date.

"'On one side of this garden slope upward the terraces of the Mount of Olives--terraces that are cultivated to-day even as the slopes of Olivet have been cultivated for generations and centuries. The other side of the garden looks toward the eastern wall of Jerusalem. Deep down in its shadowy bed, between the wall and the garden, lies the ravine of the Kedron.

"'If you visit that garden and look upon its old olive trees, the keeper of the place will tell you that you are in Gethsemane, the spot of our Saviour's betrayal. He will point out the "Grotto of the Agony," the place where the disciples slumbered, and that where Judas, before his brethren, ceased publicly to be a follower and became the betrayer of Jesus. Some things you very naturally may question as the guardian of the enclosure tells his story. Whether any one of the venerable olive trees ever threw its shadow across the prostrate form of Jesus is more than doubtful, but that these trees are burdened with the history of centuries all must concede. "Gethsemane" means "oil-press," and olive trees long ago gave Olivet its name. That somewhere in this neighborhood the Saviour suffered cannot be doubted, and within that closed wall may have been the very spot where he bowed in his agony, and where he heard the tongue of Judas utter his treacherous "Rabbi!" and where he felt the serpent-breath of the traitor as that traitor kissed him.'"

Miss Harson read of this solemn spot in a low, reverent tone; and the little audience were very quiet, until at last Clara said,

"Whenever we see an ash tree or olives, how much there will be to think of!"

CHAPTER VII.

THE USEFUL BIRCH.

"Oh, Miss Harson!" called out Clara, in great excitement, as she caught up with her governess on a run; "hasn't Edie poisoned herself? She has been eating this twig."

Edith, of course, at once began to cry.

"You are not poisoned, dear," said Miss Harson, very quickly, after trying the twig herself; "for this is birch-wood, and it cannot possibly hurt you. But remember, Edie, that this must not happen again; never put anything to your mouth unless you know it to be harmless. The birds and squirrels and other animals that are obliged to pick up their own living as soon as they are able to use their limbs have the faculty given them of knowing what is good for them to eat, but little girls are not intended to live in the woods, and they cannot tell whether or not the things they find there are fit to eat."

"I took only a little bit," sobbed Edith; "Clara snatched it away as soon as it tasted good."

Malcolm laughingly tossed his little sister into a sort of evergreen cradle where the branches grew low--for they were enjoying an afternoon in the woods--and held her there securely, while their governess replied,

"'A little bit' is too much of a thing that might be harmful. You must remember to 'touch not, taste not, handle not,' until you have asked permission. But I am going to let you all chew as many birch-shoots as you want, and I too shall chew some; for when I was a little girl, I used to think they were 'puffickly d'licious.'"

The children were much amazed to think that Miss Harson had ever talked like Edith--indeed, the two older ones could scarcely believe that they once did so themselves; but all soon had their hands full of birch-twigs, and they began gnawing like so many squirrels. All approved of the "birchskin," as Edith called it, and Malcolm declared that "it would be grand fun to live in the woods all the time."

"Couldn't we have a tent, Miss Harson," asked Clara, "and try it?"

"I have no doubt," was the reply, "that your indulgent papa would have a tent put up here for you if he thought it would make you happier, but I have my doubts as to whether it would do so. In the first place, I should object very much to living in the tent with you, and how could you possibly live there alone?"

Clara and Edith were quite sure that they could not get along without their friend and governess, but Malcolm thought he would like to try being a hermit or an Indian, he was not quite ready to say which.

"While you are deciding," said Miss Harson, with a smile, "it may be as well for us to go on as usual; but I think that a little tent could be put up here somewhere, which we might enjoy for an hour or so on pleasant days. I will see about it."

The little girls were delighted, and Malcolm finally condescended to be pleased with the idea.

"This is a very young birch," continued their governess, "and you see how slender and graceful it is; also that the bark, or 'skin,' is very dark. For this reason it is called the black, or cherry, birch, and also because the tree is very much like the black cherry. It is also called sweet birch and mahogany birch; the sweet part you can probably understand, and it gets its other name from the color of the wood, which often resembles mahogany and at one time was much used for furniture. There are larger trees of the same kind all around us, and I should like to know if anything else has been noticed besides the twigs of this little one."

"I see something," replied Malcolm: "there are flowers--purple and yellow."

"And what is the particular name for these tree-blossoms?" asked Miss Harson.

"Isn't it catkins?" inquired Clara, timidly.

"Yes, catkins, or aments. They hang, as you see, like long tassels of purple and gold, and are as fragrant as the bark. Bryant's line,

"'The fragrant birch above him hung her tassels in the sky,'

"was written of this same black birch. Some of these trees are sixty or seventy feet high, and all are very graceful, this species being considered the most beautiful of the numerous birch family. The leaves, which are just coming out, are two or three inches long and about half as wide; they taper to a point and have serrate, or sawlike, edges. The wood is firm and durable, and is much used for cattle-yokes as well as for bedsteads and chairs. The large trees yield a great quantity of sweetish sap, which makes a pleasant drink. The trees are tapped just as the sugar-maples are, and in some parts of the country gathering this sap, which is sometimes used to make vinegar, is quite an important event."

"Oh! oh! oh!" screamed Edith, and began to run.

"Oh! oh! oh!" echoed Clara; and Malcolm declared that she was just like "Jill," who "came tumbling after."

"What is the matter, children?" asked their governess, in dismay; but she stood perfectly still.

"Only a poor little garter-snake," said Malcolm, "putting his head out to see if it's warm enough for him yet. But he has gone back into his hole frightened to death at such dreadful noises. Hello! what's the matter with Edie now?"

The little sister had fallen, tripped up by some rough roots, and, expecting the poor startled garter-snake to come and make a meal off her, she was calling loudly for help.

Miss Harson had her in her arms in a moment, and it was soon found that one foot had quite a bad bruise.

"If only you had not run away!" said her governess. "He was such an innocent little snake to make all this fuss about, and very pretty too, if you had stopped to look at him."

"Are snakes ever pretty?" asked Edith, in great surprise.

"Certainly they are, dear, and this one had lovely stripes. I wish you could have seen him."

The little girl began to wish so too, it was so funny to think of a snake being pretty, and she felt quite ashamed that she had scampered away in such a silly fashion.

"What a goose I was!" said Clara, doing her thinking aloud. "But I thought it must be something dreadful, when Edie screamed so."

"How much better it would have been to have found out before you screamed!" replied Miss Harson.--"But come, Edith; see what a nice cane Malcolm has just cut to help your lame foot with. He is offering you his arm, too, on the other side, and between the two I think you will get along finely."

Edith thought the same thing, and enjoyed being helped home in this fashion. Her foot was quite painful, though, and considerably swollen; and Clara bathed it with arnica when the little girl had been comfortably established on the schoolroom sofa.

"Perhaps," said Miss Harson, "our little invalid will not care to hear about trees this evening?"

But the little invalid did care, and it was decided to take a further ramble among the birches.

"I want to hear about birch-bark," said Malcolm--"not the kind we've been eating, but the kind that canoes and things are made of."

"You have already heard about the black birch," replied his governess, "and, besides this, we have the white, or gray, birch, the bark of which is white, chalky and dotted with black; the red birch, with bark of a reddish or chocolate color; the yellow birch, bark yellowish, with a silvery lustre; and the canoe birch, which has a white bark with a pearly lustre. There is also a dwarf, or shrub, birch. The list, you see, is quite a long one."

"What kind grow in our woods?" asked Clara.

"You certainly know of one kind," was the reply--"the black, or sweet, birch, which we have all tried and like so well. Besides this, there is the white, or little gray, birch, which is seldom over twenty-five or thirty feet high. It is, however, a graceful and beautiful object, enjoying to an eminent decree the lightness and airiness of the birch family, and spreading out its glistening leaves on the ends of a very slender and often pensile spray with an indescribable softness. An English poet has called this tree the "'most beautiful Of forest-trees, the lady of the woods.'"

The children laughed at the idea of calling a tree a lady, it seemed so comical; but Miss Harson said that she thought this was a very good description of a slender, graceful tree.

"Four or five inches," she continued, "will span its waist, or trunk, and this seems a very good reason for calling it little. Another name for this tree is poplar birch, because the triangular-shaped leaves, which taper to a very long, slender point, have a habit of trembling like those of the poplars. The branches are of a dark chocolate color which contrasts very prettily with the grayish-white trunk, and their extreme slenderness causes them to droop somewhat like those of the willow. The white birch will spring up in the poorest kind of soil, and it is found in the highest latitude in which any tree can live. Its leaf is 'deltoid' in shape and indented at the edge. The bark of this species is said to be more durable than any other vegetable substance, and a piece of birch-wood was once found changed into stone, while the outer bark, white and shining, remained in its natural state,"

"I don't see how it could," said Malcolm. "What kept it from turning into stone too?"

"Its peculiar nature," was the reply, "which is a thing that we cannot explain, and we shall have to take the story just as it is. We certainly know that the wood has been proved to be very strong, and it is much used for timber."

"Is the red birch really red, Miss Harson?" asked Clara, who thought that this promised to be the prettiest member of the family.

"The bark has a reddish tinge, and it is so loose and ragged-looking that it has been said to roll up its bark in coarse ringlets, which are whitish with a stain of crimson. The red birch, which is more rare than any of the other kinds, is a much larger tree than the white birch, but, like all its relations, it is very graceful. The wood is white and hard and makes very good fuel, while the twigs are made into brooms for sweeping streets and courtyards."

"But there isn't very much red about it, after all," said Malcolm.

"It wasn't red," murmured Edith; "it was green;" and the next moment "the baby" was fast asleep, but Miss Harson was afraid that she had taken the snake with her to the land of Nod, so restless was her sleep.

"I hope the yellow birch is yellow," said Clara again.

"We will see what is said of its color," replied her governess, "and here it is: 'Distinguished by its yellowish bark, of a soft silken texture and silvery or pearly lustre,' It is a large tree, and has been named excelsa--'lofty'--because of its height. The slender, flowing branches are very graceful, and the tree is often as symmetrical as a fine elm, but droops less. The roots of the yellow birch seem to enjoy getting above the ground and twisting themselves in a very fantastic manner, and, taken altogether, it is a strikingly handsome and ornamental tree. The wood was at one time much liked for fuel, and many of the logs were of immense size."

"Now," said Malcolm, gleefully, "the canoe birch has got to come next, because there isn't anything else to come."

"That is an excellent reason," replied Miss Harson, "and the canoe birch it shall be. There is more to be said of it than of any of the others, and it also grows in greater quantities. Thick woods of it are found in Maine and New Hampshire--for it loves a cold climate--and in other Northern portions of the country. The tall trunks of the trees resemble pillars of polished marble supporting a canopy of bright-green foliage. The leaves are something of a heart-shape, and their vivid summer green turns to golden tints in autumn. The bark of the canoe birch is almost snowy white on the outside, and very prettily marked with fine brown stripes two or three inches long, which go around the trunk. This bark is very smooth and soft, and it is easily separated into very thin sheets. For this reason the tree is often called the paper birch, and the smooth, thin layers of bark make very good writing-paper when none other can be had."

"Oh, Miss Harson!" exclaimed Clara; "did you ever see any that was written on?"

"Yes," was the reply; "I once wrote a letter on some myself."

"Did you really?" cried two eager voices. "How could you? Oh, do tell us about it!"

"I was making a visit at a village in Maine," said their governess, "where the beautiful trees are to be seen in all their perfection, and I thought it would be appropriate to write a letter from there on birch bark. So I split my bark very thin and got a respectable sheet of it ready; then I cut another piece, to form an envelope, and gummed it together. I had quite a struggle to write on it decently with a steel pen, because the pen would go through the paper; but I persevered, and finally I accomplished my letter. It seemed odd to put a postage-stamp on birch bark, and I smiled to think how surprised the home-people would be to get such a letter. They were surprised, and they told me afterward that the postman laughed when he delivered it."

The children thought this very interesting, and they wished that there were canoe-birch trees growing at Elmridge, that they might be enabled to try the experiment for themselves.

"Now," continued Miss Harson, "I am going to read you an account of canoe-making, and of some other uses to which the bark is put:

"'In Canada and in the district of Maine the country-people place large pieces of the bark immediately below the shingles of the roof, to form a more impenetrable covering for their houses. Baskets, boxes and portfolios are made of it, which are sometimes embroidered with silk of different colors. Divided into very thin sheets, it forms a substitute for paper, and placed between the soles of the shoes and in the crown of the hat it is a defence against dampness. But the most important purpose to which it is applied, and one in which it is replaced by the bark of no other tree, is in the construction of canoes. To procure proper pieces, the largest and smoothest trunks are selected. In the spring two circular incisions are made, several feet apart, and two longitudinal ones on opposite sides of the tree; after which, by introducing a wooden wedge, the bark is easily detached. These plates are usually ten or twelve feet long and two feet nine inches broad. To form the canoe, they are stitched together with fibrous roots of the white spruce about the size of a quill, which are deprived of the bark, split and suppled in water. The seams are coated with resin of the balm of Gilead.

"'Great use is made of these canoes by the savages and by the French Canadians in their long journeys into the interior of the country; they are very light, and are easily transported on the shoulders from one lake or river to another, which is called the portage. A canoe calculated for four persons, with their baggage, weighs from forty to fifty pounds; some of them are made to carry fifteen passengers.'

"And now let me show you a picture of the Kentucky pioneer in a birch-bark canoe."

"Why, Miss Harson, the Indians are trying to kill him!" exclaimed Malcolm.

"Yes," she replied; "when you read the history of the United States, you will find that not only Daniel Boone, but the most of the early settlers of these Western lands, had trouble with the Indians. Nor is this strange. These pioneers were often rough men, and were looked upon by the natives as invaders of their country and treated as enemies. But to come back to the uses of the bark of the birch:

"'In the settlements of the Hudson Bay Company tents are made of the bark of this tree, which for that purpose is cut into pieces twelve feet long and four feet wide. These are sewed together by threads made of the white-spruce roots; and so rapidly is a tent put up that a circular one twenty feet in diameter and ten feet high does not occupy more than half an hour in pitching. Every traveler and hunter in Canada enjoys these "rind-tents," as they are called, which are used only during the hot summer months, when they are found particularly comfortable.'"

"Well, that's the funniest thing yet!" exclaimed Malcolm. "'Rind-tents'! I wish I could see one. Did they have any in Maine where you were, Miss Harson?"

"No," was the reply, "I did not even hear of such a thing there, and to see it you would probably have to go far to the north. The English birch, which is found also in many parts of Europe, is put to a great many uses; the leaves produce a yellow dye, and the wood, when mixed with copperas, will color red, black and brown. An old birch tree that is supposed to be giving an account of itself says,

"'How many are the uses of my bark! Thrifty men who sit beside the blazing hearth when my branches throw up a clear bright flame, and follow the example of their fathers in making their own shoes and those of their families, tan the hides with my bark. Kamschadales construct from it both hats and vessels for holding milk, and the Swedish fisherman his shoes. The Norwegian covers with it his low-roofed hut and spreads upon the surface layers of moss at least three or four inches thick, and, having twisted long strips together, he obtains excellent torches with which to cheer the darkness of his long nights. Fishermen, in like manner, make great use of them in alluring their finny prey. For this purpose they fit a portion of blazing birch in a cleft stick and spear the fish when attracted by its flickering light.'"

The children exclaimed at this queer way of fishing, but Malcolm was very much taken with the idea of doing it by night with blazing torches, and he thought that he would like to be a Norwegian fisherman even better than a hermit or an Indian.

"The old tree goes on to say," continued Miss Harson, "that 'Finland mothers form of the dried leaves soft, elastic beds for their children, and from me is prepared the mona, their sole medicine in all diseases. My buds in spring exhale a delicious fragrance after showers, and the bark, when burnt, seems to purify the air in confined dwellings.'

"In Lapland the twigs of the birch, covered with reindeer-skins, are used for beds, but they cannot be so comfortable, I should think, as the leaves. The fragrant wood of the tree makes the fires which have to be kept up inside the huts even in summer to drive away the mosquitoes, and the people of those Northern regions would find it hard to get along without the useful birch."

"I like to hear about it," said Clara. "Can you tell us something more that is done with it, Miss Harson?"

"There is just one thing more," replied her governess, with a smile, "which I will read out of an old book; and I desire you all to pay particular attention to it."

Little Edith was wide awake again by this time, and her great blue eyes looked as if she were ready to devour every word.

"Birch rods," continued Miss Harson, "are quite different from birch twigs, and the uses to which they were put were not altogether agreeable to the boys who ran away from school or did not get their lessons. 'My branches,' says the birch, 'gently waving in the wind, awakened in those days no feelings of dread with truant urchins--for all might be truants then, if so it pleased them--but at length a scribe arose who thus wrote concerning my ductile twigs: "The civil uses whereunto the birch serveth are many, as for the punishment of children both at home and abroad; for it hath an admirable influence upon them to quiet them when they wax unruly, and therefore some call the tree make-peace"'" Malcolm and Clara both laughed, and asked their young governess when the birch rods were coming; but Edith did not feel quite so easy, and, with her bruised foot and all, it took a great deal of petting that night to get her comfortably to bed.

CHAPTER VIII.

THE POPLARS.

The bruised foot was not comfortable to walk on for two or three days, and Edith was settled in the great easy arm-chair with dolls and toys and picture-books in a pile that seemed as if it would not stop growing until every article belonging to herself and Clara had been gathered there. "We can go on with our trees," said Miss Harson, "even if we do not see them just yet; and this evening I should like to tell you something about the poplar, a large tree with alternate leaves which is often found in dusty towns, where it seems to flourish as well as in its favorite situation by a running stream. An old English writer calls the poplars 'hospitable trees, for anything thrives under their shade.' They are not handsomely-shaped trees, but the foliage is thick and pretty. In the latter part of this month--April--the trees are so covered with their olive-green catkins that large portions of the forests seem to be colored by them."

"Are there any poplars at Elmridge?" asked Malcolm.

"Not nearer than the woods," was the reply, "where we must go and look for them when Edith's foot is quite well again, though there are a good many in the city. The poplar is often planted by the roadside because it grows so rapidly and makes a good shade. The Abele, or silver poplar, is an especial favorite for this purpose.

"The balm of Gilead, or Canada poplar, is the largest of the species, and really a handsome tree, often growing to the height of fifty or sixty feet, with a trunk of proportionate size. It has large leaves of a bright, glossy green, which grow loosely on long branches, A peculiarity of this tree is that before the leaves begin to expand the buds are covered with a yellow, glutinous balsam that diffuses a penetrating but very agreeable odor unlike any other. The balsam is gathered as a healing anodyne, and for many ailments it is a favorite remedy in domestic medicine. All the poplars produce more or less of this substance.

"The river poplaris found on the banks of rivers and brooks and in wet places, and is a noble and graceful tree. The trunk is light gray in color, and the young trees have a smooth, leather-like bark. The broad leaves, of a very rich green, grow on stems nearly as long as themselves, and the flowering aments are of a light-red color. The leaf-stalks and young branches are also brightly tinted. Another of these trees has a very singular name: it is called the necklace poplar."

"Do the flowers grow like real necklaces?" asked Clara.

"Not quite," replied her governess, "but the reason given is something like it. The tree is so called from the resemblance of the long ament, before opening, to the beads of a necklace. In Europe it is known as the Swiss poplar and the black Italian poplar. Its timber is much valued there for building. There are also the black poplar and that queer, stiff-looking tree the Lombardy poplar. Cannot one of you tell me where there are some tall, narrow trees that look almost as if they had been cut out of wood and stuck there?"

"I know where there are some," said Malcolm: "right in front of Mrs. Bush's old house; and I think they're miserable-looking trees."

"When old and rusty, they are not in the least cheerful," replied Miss

Harson; "and it is so long since Lombardy poplars were admired that few are found except about old places. The tree is shaped like a tall spire, and in hot, calm weather drops of clear water trickle from its leaves like a slight shower of rain. It was once a favorite shade-tree, and a century ago great numbers of Lombardy poplars were planted by village waysides, in front of dwelling-houses, on the borders of public grounds, and particularly in avenues leading to houses that stand at some distance from the high-road.

"The poplar is found in many lands. The Lombardy poplar, as its name indicates, was brought from Italy, where it grows luxuriantly beside the orange and the myrtle; but after one of our cold winters many of its small branches will decay, and this gives it a forlorn appearance. When fresh and green, the Lombardy poplar is quite handsome. Some one wrote of it long ago: 'There is no other tree that so pleasantly adorns the sides of narrow lanes and avenues, and so neatly accommodates itself to limited enclosures. Its foliage is dense and of the liveliest verdure, making delicate music to the soft touch of every breeze. Its terebinthine odors scent the vernal gales that enter our open windows with the morning sun. Its branches, always turning upward and closely gathered together, afford a harbor to the singing-birds that make them a favorite resort, and its long, tapering spire that points to heaven gives an air of cheerfulness and religious tranquillity to village scenery.'"

"I wish we had some," said Edith, "with singing-birds in 'em."

"Why, my dear child," replied her governess, "have we not the beautiful elms, in which the birds build their nests and where they fly in and out continually? They are the very same birds that build in the Lombardy poplars."

"I thought that singing-birds always lived in cages," said the little queen in the easy-chair.

"And did you think they were hung all over the Lombardy poplars?" asked Malcolm, in a broad grin.

Edith laughed too, and Miss Harson said smilingly.

"I thought that the birds about Elmridge did a great deal of singing, and the blue-birds and robins kept it up all day. But I should not like to see the old Lombardy poplars hung with gilded cages, and the birds which should happen to be prisoners in the cages would like it still less."

"Well," said Edith, contentedly, as she settled herself again to listen.

"The poplar," continued Miss Harson, "has a great many insect enemies, and the Lombardy is not often seen now, because a great many of these trees were destroyed on account of a worm, or caterpillar, by which they were infested. Poplar-wood is soft, light and generally of a pale-yellow color; it is much used for toy-making and for boarded floors, 'for which last purpose it is well adapted from its whiteness and the facility with which it is scoured, and also from the difficulty with which it catches fire and the slowness with which it burns. A red-hot poker falling on a board of poplar would burn its way without causing more combustion than the hole through which it passed.'"

"I should think, then," said Malcolm, "that all wooden things would be made of poplar."

"It is generally thought not to be durable," was the reply, "but it is said that if kept dry the wood will last as long as that of any tree. Says the poplar plank,

"'Though heart of oak be ne'er so stout, Keep me dry and I'll see him out.'

"The poplar has been highly praised, for every part of this tree answers some good purpose. The bark, being light, like cork, serves to support the nets of fishermen; the inner bark is used by the Kamschadales as a material for bread; brooms are made from the twigs, and paper from the cottony down of the seeds. Horses, cows and sheep browse upon it.

"And now," said Miss Harson, when the children were wondering if that were the end, "we have come to the most interesting tree of the whole species--the aspen, or trembling poplar. It is a small, graceful tree with rounded leaves having a wavy, toothed border, covered with soft silk when young, which remains only as a fringe on the edge at maturity, supported by a very slender footstalk about as long as the leaf, and compressed laterally from near the base. They are thus agitated by the slightest breath of wind with that quivering, restless motion characteristic of all the poplars, but in none so striking as this. 'To quiver like an aspen-leaf has become a proverb. The foliage appears lighter than that of most other trees, from continually displaying the under side of the leaves.

"The aspen has been called a very poetical tree, because it is the only one whose leaves tremble when the wind is apparently calm. It is said, however, to suggest fickleness and caprice, levity and irresolution--a bad character for any tree. The small American aspen, which is quite common, has a smooth, pale-green bark, which gets whitish and rough as the tree grows old. The foliage is thin, but a single leaf will be found, when examined, uncommonly beautiful. A spray of the small aspen, when in leaf, is very light and airy-looking, and the leaves produce a constant rustling sound. 'Legends of no ordinary interest linger around this tree. Ask the Italian peasant who pastures his sheep beside a grove of Abele why the leaves of these trees are always trembling in even the hottest weather when not a breeze is stirring, and he will tell you that the wood of the trembling-poplar formed the cross on which our Saviour suffered.'"

"Oh, Miss Harson!" said Clara, in a low tone. "Is that true?"

"We do not know that it is, dear, nor do we know that it is not. Here are some verses about it which I like very much:

"'The tremulousness began, as legends tell, When he, the meek One, bowed his head to death E'en on an aspen cross, when some near dell Was visited by men whose every breath That Sufferer gave them. Hastening to the wood-- The wood of aspens--they with ruffian power Did hew the fair, pale tree, which trembling stood As if awestruck; and from that fearful hour Aspens have quivered as with conscious dread Of that foul crime which bowed the meek Redeemer's head.

"'Far distant from those days, oh let not man, Boastful of reason, check with scornful speech Those legends pure; for who the heart may scan Or say what hallowed thoughts such legends teach To those who may perchance their scant flocks keep On hill or plain, to whom the quivering tree Hinteth a thought which, holy, solemn, deep, Sinks in the heart, bidding their spirits flee All thoughts of vice, that dread and hateful thing Which troubleth of each joy the pure and gushing spring?'"

CHAPTER IX.

ALL A-BLOW: THE APPLE TREE.

It certainly was a beautiful sight, and the children exclaimed over it in ectasy. It was now past the middle of April, and Miss Harson had taken her little flock to visit an apple-orchard at some distance from Elmridge, and the whole place seemed to be one mass of pink-and-white bloom.

"And how deliciously sweet it is!" said Malcolm as he sniffed the fragrant air.

"Oh!" exclaimed Edith, turning up her funny little nose to get the full benefit of all this fragrance; "I can't breathe half enough at once."

"That is just my case," said her governess, laughing, "but I did not think to say it in that way. Get all you can of this deliciousness, children; I wish that we could carry some of it away with us."

"And so you shall," replied a hearty voice as Mr. Grove, the owner of the orchard, came up with a knife in his hand and began cutting off small branches of apple--blossoms. "I like to see folks enjoy things."

"I hope you don't mind our trespassing on your grounds?" said Miss Harson. "I can engage that my little friends will do no injury, and I particularly wished them to see your beautiful orchard in bloom; it is almost equal to a field of roses."

"Don't mind it at all, miss," was the reply--"quite the contrary; and I think, myself, it's a pretty sight. Smells good, too. Now, here's a nosegay big enough for you three young ladies, and Bub there can carry it."

Malcolm, who was quite proud of his name, felt so indignant at being called "Bub" that he almost forgot the farmer's generosity; but his governess acknowledged it, very much to the worthy man's satisfaction.

Edith, however, was rather shocked.

"I thought it was wicked," said she, "to cut off flowers from fruit trees? Won't these make apples?"

"Not them particular ones, Sis," replied Mr. Grove, with a laugh; "they're done for now. But it ain't wicked to cut off your own apple blows when there's too many on the tree to make good apples, and there's plenty to spare yet." He was very much amused at the little girl's serious face over this wholesale destruction of infant apples, and he invited them all to come to the house and get a drink of fresh milk. The children thought this a very pleasant invitation, and Miss Harson was quite willing to gratify them.

The farmer led his guests into a very cheerful and wonderfully clean kitchen, where Mrs. Groves was busy with her baking, and the loaves of fresh bread looked very inviting. She was as pleasant and hospitable as her husband, and after shaking up a funny-looking patchwork cushion in a rocking-chair for the young lady to sit down on she told the little girls that she would get them a couple of crickets if they would wait a minute, and disappeared into the next room.

The two little sisters looked at each other in dismay and wondered what they could do with these insects, but before they could consult Miss Harson good Mrs. Grove had returned carrying in each hand a small flat footstool. The girls sat down very carefully, for they were not accustomed to such low seats; but the whole party were tired with their walk and glad to rest for a short time. Malcolm, being a boy, was expected to sit where he could, and he speedily established himself in the corner of a wooden settle.

In spite of the apple-blossoms, the kitchen fire was very comfortable; and, as the baking was just coming to an end, Mrs.

Grove said that "she would be ready to visit with them in a minute:" she did not seem to allow herself more than a "minute" for anything. Besides the milk, some very nice seed-cakes in the shape of hearts were produced, and Edith thought them the most delightful little cakes she had ever tasted. Clara and Malcolm, too, were quite hungry, and Miss Harson enjoyed her glass of milk and seed-cake as well as did the young people. The farmer and his wife seemed really sorry to part with their guests when they rose to go, but Miss Harson said that it was time for them to be at home, and the children were obedient on the instant.

"Well," said the worthy couple, "you know now where to come when you want more apple-blows and a drink of milk."

Malcolm was quite laden with the mass of rosy flowers which Mr. Grove piled up in his arms, and he enjoyed the delicious scent all the way home.

"I must get out the big jar," said Miss Harson as she surveyed their treasures, "and there are so many buds that I think we may be able to keep them for some days.--What would you say, Edith, if I told you that people cut off not only the blossoms, but even the fruit itself, while it is green, to make what is left on the tree handsomer and better?"

Edith looked her surprise, and the other children could not understand why all the fruit that formed should not be left on the tree to ripen.

"It is very often left," replied their governess, "but, although the crop is a large one, it will be of inferior quality; and those who understand fruit-raising thin it out, so that the tree may not have more fruit than it can well nourish. But now it is time for papa to come, and after dinner we will have a regular apple-talk."

"How nice it was at Mrs. Grove's to-day!" said Clara, when they were gathered for the talk. "I think that kitchens are pleasanter to sit in than parlors and school-rooms."

"So do I," chimed in Edith; "but I was afraid about the crickets at first. I thought we'd have to hold 'em in our hands, and I didn't like that."

Why would people always laugh when there was nothing to laugh at? The little girl thought she had a very funny brother and sister, and Miss Harson, too, was funny sometimes.

"Have you so soon forgotten about the real insect-crickets, dear?" asked her governess, kindly. "Why, it will be months yet before we see one. Besides,

I thought I told you that in some places a little bench is called a 'cricket'?--Do you know, Clara, why you thought Mrs. Grove's kitchen so pleasant? It is larger and better furnished than kitchens usually are, there were pleasant people in it, and you were tired and hungry and ready to enjoy rest and refreshments; but I am quite sure that, on the whole, you would like your own quarters best, because you are better fitted for them, as Mrs. Grove is for hers. We had a very pleasant visit, though, and some day we may repeat it--perhaps when the apples are ripe."

"Good! good!" cried the children, clapping their hands; and Malcolm added that he "would like to be let loose in that apple-orchard."

"Perhaps you would like it better than Farmer Grove would," was the reply. "But we haven't got to the apples yet; we must first find out a little about the tree. We learn in the beginning that it was one of the very earliest trees planted in this country by the settlers, because it is both hardy and useful. There is a wild species called the Virginia crab-apple, which bears beautiful pink flowers as fragrant as roses, but its small apples are intensely sour. The blossoms of the cultivated apple tree are more beautiful than those of any other fruit; they are delicious to both sight and scent."

"And do look, Miss Harson," said Clara, "at these lovely half-open buds! They are just like tiny roses, and so sweet!"

Down went Clara's head among the clustered blossoms, and then Edith had to come too; and Malcolm declared that between the two they would smell them to death.

"It seems," continued Miss Harson, "that the apple tree grows wild in every part of Europe except in the frigid zone and in Western Asia, China and Japan. It is thought to have been planted in Britain by the Romans; and when it was brought here, it seemed to do better than it had done anywhere else. It is said that 'not only the Indians, but many indigenous insects, birds and quadrupeds, welcomed the apple tree to these shores. The butterfly of the tent-caterpillar saddled her eggs on the very first twig that was formed, and it has since shared her affections with the wild cherry; and the canker-worm also, in a measure, abandoned the elm to feed on it. As it grew apace the bluebird, robin, cherry-bird, king-bird, and many more, came with haste and built their nests and warbled in its boughs, and so became orchard-birds and multiplied more than ever. It was an era in the history of their race in America. The downy woodpecker found such a savory morsel under its bark that he perforated it in a ring quite round the tree before he left it. It did not take the partridge long to find out how sweet its buds were, and every winter eve she flew, and still flies, from the wood to pluck them, much to the farmer's sorrow. The rabbit, too, was not slow to learn the taste of its twigs and bark; and when the fruit was ripe, the squirrel half rolled, half carried, it to his hole. Even the musquash crept up the bank from the brook at evening, and greedily devoured it, until he had worn a path in the grass there; and when it was frozen and thawed, the crow and the jay were glad to taste it occasionally. The owl crept into the first apple tree that became hollow, and fairly hooted with delight, finding it just the place for him; so, settling down into it, he has remained there ever since.'

"Speaking of these buds, Clara," said her governess, "I think I forgot to tell you that the apple tree belongs to the family Rosaceae, and therefore the half-opened blossoms have a right to look like roses. The tree is not a handsome one, being a small edition of the oak in its sturdy outline, but it is less graceful or picturesque-looking, being often broader than it is high and resembling in shape a half globe. The leaves are not pretty except when first unfolded, and their color is then a beautiful light tint known as apple-green. But the foliage soon becomes dusty and shabby-looking. An old apple tree, with its gnarled, and often hollow, trunk, is generally handsomer than a young one, unless in the time of blossoms; for only a young apple-orchard is covered with such a profusion of bloom as that we saw to-day."

"I am glad," said Clara, "that it belongs to the rose family, for now the dear little buds seem prettier than ever."

"The apples are prettier yet," observed

Malcolm; "if there's anything I like, it's apples."

"I am afraid that you eat too many of them for your good," replied his governess; "I shall have to limit you to so many a day."

"I have eaten only six to-day," was the modest reply, "and they were little russets, too."

"Oh, Malcolm, Malcolm!" said Miss Harson, laughing; "what shall I do with you? Why, you would soon make an apple-famine in most places. Three apples a day must be your allowance for the present; and if at any time we go to live in an orchard, you may have six."

"Why, we have only one," exclaimed little Edith, "and we don't want any more.--Do we, Clara?"

[Illustration: Apple Blossoms.]

"If you don't want 'em," said Malcolm, "there's no sense in eating 'em.--But I'll remember, Miss Harson. I suppose three at one time ought to be enough."

Malcolm's expression, as he said this, was so doleful that every one laughed at him; and his governess continued:

"The apple tree is said to produce a greater variety of beautiful fruit than any other tree that is known, and apples are liked by almost every one. They are a very wholesome fruit and nearly as valuable as bread and potatoes for food, because they can be used in so many different ways, and the poorer qualities make very nourishing food for nearly all animals."

"Rex fairly snatches the apple out of my hand when I go to give him one," said Malcolm.

"So does Regina," added Clara, who trembled in her shoes whenever she offered these dainties to the handsome carriage-horses.

Edith had not dared to venture on such a feat yet, and therefore she had nothing to say.

"All horses are fond of apples," said Miss Harson, "and the fruit is very thoroughly appreciated. Ancient Britain was celebrated for her apple-orchards, and the tree was reverenced by the Druids because the mistletoe grew abundantly on it. In Saxon times, when England became a Christian country, the rite of coronation, or crowning of a king, was in such words as these: 'May the almighty Lord give thee, O king, from the dew of heaven and the fatness of the earth, abundance of corn and wine and oil! Be thou the lord of thy brothers, and let the sons of thy mother bow down before thee. Let the people serve thee and the tribes adore thee. May the Almighty bless thee with the blessings of heaven above, and the mountains and the valleys with the blessings of the deep below, with the blessings of grapes and apples! Bless, O Lord, the courage of this prince, and prosper the work of his hands; and by thy blessing may his land be filled with apples, with the fruit and dew of heaven from the top of the ancient mountains, from the apples of the eternal hills, from the fruit of the earth and its fullness!' You will see from this how highly apples were valued in England in those ancient times."

"I should like to pick them up when they are ripe," said Clara, and Malcolm expressed a desire to hire himself out by the day to Mr. Grove when that time arrived.

"An apple-orchard in autumn," continued their governess, "is often a merry scene. Ladders are put against the trees, and the finest apples are carefully picked off, but such as are to be used for cider-making are shaken to the ground. Men and boys are at work, and even women and children are there with baskets and aprons spread out to catch the fruit; and they run back and forth wherever the apples fall thickest, with much laughter at the unexpected showers that come down upon their heads and necks. Large baskets filled with these apples are carried to the mill, where, after being laid in heaps a while to mellow, they are crushed and pressed till their juice is extracted; and this, being fermented, becomes cider. From this cider, by a second fermentation, the best vinegar is made."

"Miss Harson," asked Edith, as the talk seemed to have come to an end, "isn't there any more about apple trees? I like 'em."

"Yes, dear," was the reply; "there is more. I was just looking over, in this little book, some queer superstitions about apple trees in England, and here is a strange performance which is said to take place in some very retired parts of the country:

"'Scarcely have the merry bells ushered in the morning of Christmas than a troop of people may be seen entering the apple-orchard, often when the trees are powdered with hoarfrost and snow lies deep upon the ground. One of the company carries a large flask filled with cider and tastefully decorated with holly-branches; and when every one has advanced about ten paces from the choicest tree, rustic pipes made from the hollow boughs of elder are played upon by young men, while Echo repeats the strain, and it seems as if fairy-musicians responded in low, sweet tones from some neighboring wood or hill. Then bursts forth a chorus of loud and sonorous voices while the cider-flask is being emptied of its contents around the tree, and all sing some such words as these:

"""Here's to thee, old apple tree! Long mayest thou grow. And long mayest thou blow, and ripen the apples that hang on thy bough!

"""This full can of apple wine, Old tree, be thine: It will cheer thee and warm thee amid the deep snow;

"""Till the goldfinch--fond bird!-- In the orchard is heard Singing blithe 'mid the blossoms that whiten thy bough."""

"But what did they do it for?" asked Malcolm, who enjoyed the account as much as the others. "There doesn't seem to be any sense in it."

"There is no sense in it," replied his governess, "but these ignorant people had inherited the custom from their fathers and grandfathers, and they really believed--and perhaps still believe--that this attention would be sure to bring a fine crop of apples. We are distinctly told, though, that 'it is God that giveth the increase;' and to him alone belong the fruits of the earth. Sometimes the crop is so great that the trees fairly bend over with the weight of the fruit, and there is an old English saying: 'The more apples the tree bears, the more she bows to the folk.'"

"How funny!" laughed Edith. "Does the apple tree move its head, Miss Harson?"

"It cannot go quite so far as that," was the reply; "it just stays bent over like a person carrying a heavy burden. The branches of overladen fruit trees are sometimes propped up with long poles to keep them from breaking. There is another strange custom, which used to be practiced on New Year's eve. It was called 'Apple-Howling,' and a troop of boys visited the different orchards--which would scarcely have been desirable when the apples were ripe--and, forming a ring around the trees, repeated these words:

"'Stand fast, root! bear well, top! Pray God send us a good howling crop--Every twig, apples big; Every bough, apples enow.'

"All then shouted in chorus, while one of the party played on a cow's horn, and the trees were well rapped with the sticks which they carried. This ceremony is thought to have been a relic of some heathen sacrifice, and it is quite absurd enough to be that."

"What is 'a howling crop,' Miss Harson?" asked Clara. "That name sounds so queer!"

"I don't know what it can be," replied her governess, "unless it refers to the strange expression sometimes used, 'howling with delight.' We hear more commonly of 'howling with pain,' but 'a howling crop' must be one that makes the owner scream, as well as dance for joy."

"Why, I scream only when I'm frightened," said Edith, who began to think that there were much sillier people in the world than herself.

"At garter-snakes," added Malcolm, giving his sister a sly pinch; but Edith did not mind his pinches, because he always took good care not to hurt her.

Miss Harson said that the best way was not to scream at all, as it was both a silly and a troublesome habit, and the sooner her charges broke themselves of it the better she should like it. Clara and Edith both promised to try--just as they had promised before, when the ants were so troublesome; but they were nine months older now, and seemed to be getting a little ashamed of the habit.

"Are apples mentioned anywhere in the Bible?" asked Miss Harson, presently.

Clara and Malcolm were busy thinking, but nothing came of it, until their governess said,

"Turn to the book of Proverbs, Clara, and find the twenty-fifth chapter and the eleventh verse."

Clara read very carefully:

"'A word fitly spoken is like apples of gold in pictures of silver.' But what does it mean?" she asked.

"It probably means 'framed in silver' or 'in silver frames[11],'" was the reply; "and then it is easy to understand how important our words are, and that 'fitly-spoken' ones are as valuable and lasting as golden apples framed in silver. The apple tree is mentioned in Joel, where it is said that 'all the trees of the field are withered[12],' and both apple trees and apples are mentioned in several places of the Old Testament. But, to tell the whole truth, scholars are not agreed as to whether the Hebrew word denotes the apple or some other fruit that grew in the land of Israel."

[11] The Revised Version renders the phrase "in baskets of silver."

[12] Joel i. 12.

The children had all enjoyed the "apple-talk," and they felt that the fruit which they were so accustomed to seeing would now have a new meaning for them.

CHAPTER X.

A FRUITFUL FAMILY: THE PEACH, ALMOND, PLUM AND CHERRY.

Snowdrops, crocuses, hyacinths and tulips were blooming out of doors and in-doors; the grass looked green and velvety, and the fruit trees were, as John expressed it, "all a-blow." The peach trees, without a sign of a leaf, looked, as every one said of them, like immense bouquets of pink flowers, while pear, cherry and plum trees seemed as if they were dressed in white.

One cloudy, windy day, when the petals fell off in showers and strewed the ground, Edith declared that it was snowing; but she soon saw her mistake, and then began to worry because there would be no blossoms left for fruit.

"If the flowers stayed on, there would be no fruit," said Miss Harson. "Let me show you just where the little green germ is."

"Why, of course!" said Malcolm; "it's in the part that stays on the tree."

Edith listened intently while her governess showed her the ovary of a blossom safe on the twig where it grew, and explained to her that it was this which, nourished by the sap of the tree, with the aid of the sun and air, would ripen into fruit, while the petals were merely a fringe or ornament to the true blossom.

At Elmridge, scattered here and there through garden and grounds, as Mr. Kyle liked to have them, there were some fruit trees of every kind that would flourish in that part of the country, but there was no orchard; and for this reason Miss Harson had taken the children to see the grand apple-blossoming at Farmer Grove's. Two very large pear trees stood one on either side of the lawn, and there were dwarf pear trees in the garden.

"I think pears are nicer than apples," said Clara as they stood looking at the fine trees, now perfectly covered with their snowy blossoms.

But Malcolm, who found it hard work to be happy on three apples a day, stoutly disagreed with his sister on this point, and declared that nothing was so good as apples.

"How about ice-cream?" asked his governess, when she heard this sweeping assertion.

The young gentleman was silent, for his exploits with this frozen luxury were a constant subject of wonder to his friends and relatives.

"You will notice," said Miss Harson, "that the shape of these trees is much more graceful than that of the apple tree. They are tall and slender, forming what is called an imperfect pyramid. Standard pear trees, like these, give a good shade, and the long, slender branches are well clothed with leaves of a bright, glossy green. This rich color lasts late into the autumn, and it is then varied with yellow, and often with red and black, spots; so that pear-leaves are not to be despised in gathering autumn-leaf treasures. The pear is not so useful a fruit as the apple, nor so showy in color; but it has a more delicate and spicy flavor, and often is of an immense size."

"Yes, indeed!" said Clara. "Don't you remember, Miss Harson, that sometimes Edith and I can have only one pear divided between us at dessert because they are so large?"

"Yes, dear; and I think that half a duchess pear is as much as can be comfortably managed at once."

"Well," observed Malcolm, "I don't want half an apple.--But, Miss Harson, do they ever have 'pear-howlings' in England?"

"I have never read of any," was the reply, "and I think that strange custom is confined to apple trees. And there is no mention made of either pears or pear trees in the Scriptures."

"What are prickly-pears?" asked Clara. "Do they have thorns on 'em?"

"There is a plant by this name," replied her governess, "with large yellow flowers, and the fruit is full of small seeds and has a crimson pulp. It grows in sandy places near the salt water; it is abundant in North Africa and Syria, and is considered quite good to eat; but neither plant nor fruit bears any resemblance to our pear trees: it is a cactus."

"Won't you have a story for us this evening, Miss Harson?" asked Edith, rather wistfully.

"Perhaps so, dear--I have been thinking of it--but it will not be about pear trees."

"Oh, I don't care," with a very bright face; "I'd as soon have it about cherry trees, or--'Most anything!"

Miss Harson laughed, and said,

"Well, then, I think it will be about cherries; so you must rest on that. This morning we will go around among the fruit trees and see what we can learn from seeing them."

Of course it was Saturday morning and there were no lessons, or they would not have been roaming around "promiscuous," as Jane called it; for the young governess was very careful not to let the getting of one kind of knowledge interfere with the getting of another.

"How do you like these pretty quince trees?" asked Miss Harson as they came to some large bushes with great pinkish flowers.

"I like 'em," replied Edith, "because they're so little. And oh what pretty flowers!"

"Some more relations of the rose," said her governess. "And do you notice how fragrant they are? The tree is always low and crooked, just as you see it, and the branches straggle not very gracefully. The under part of the dark-green leaves is whitish and downy-looking, and the flowers are handsome enough to warrant the cultivation of the tree just for their sake, but the large golden fruit is much prized for preserves, and in the autumn a small tree laden down with it is quite an ornamental object. The quince is more like a pear than an apple. As the book says, 'it has the same tender and mucilaginous core; the seeds are not enclosed in a dry hull, like those of the apple; and the pulp of the quince, like that of the pear, is granulated, while that of the apple displays in its texture a firmer and finer organization.' The fruit, however, is so hard, even when ripe, that it cannot be eaten without cooking. It is said to be a native of hedges and rocky places in the South of Europe."

"These peach trees," said Clara, "look like sticks with pink flowers all over 'em." "They are remarkably bare of leaves when in bloom," was the reply: "the leaves burst forth from their envelopes as the blossoms pass away; but how beautiful the blossoms are! from the deepest pink to that delicate tint which is called peach-color. But do you know that we have left the apple and rose family now, and have come to the almond family?"

The children were very much surprised to hear this, and they looked at the peach trees with fresh interest.

"Yes," continued Miss Harson, "the family consists of the almond tree, the peach tree, the apricot tree, the plum tree and the cherry tree; and one thing that distinguishes them from the other families is the gum which is found on their trunks.--Look around, Malcolm, at the peach, plum and cherry trees, which are the only members of the family that we have at Elmridge, and you will find gum oozing from the bark, especially where there are knotholes."

Malcolm not only found the gum, but succeeded in helping himself to some of it, which he shared with his sisters. It had a rather sweet taste, and the children seemed to like it, having first obtained permission of their governess to eat it.

"That is another of the things that I thought 'puffickly d'licious' when I was a child," said the young lady, laughing. "But there is another peculiarity of this family of trees which is not so innocent, and that is that in the fruit-kernel, and also in the leaves, there is a deadly poison called prussic acid."

"O--h!" exclaimed the children, drawing back from the trees as though they expected to be poisoned on the spot.

"But, as we do not eat either the kernels or the leaves," continued their governess, "we need not feel uneasy, for the fruit never yet poisoned any one. Here are the cherry trees, so covered with blossoms that they look like masses of snow; and the smaller plum trees are also attired in white. We will begin this evening with the almond tree, and see what we can find out about the family."

"Do almond trees and peach trees look alike?" asked Clara, when they were fairly settled by the schoolroom fire; for the evenings were too cool yet for the piazza.

"Very much alike," was the reply; "only the almond tree is larger and it has white instead of pink blossoms. Then it is the fruit of the peach we eat, but of the almond we eat the kernel of the stem. I will read you a little account of it:

"'The common almond is a native of Barbary, but has long been cultivated in the South of Europe and the temperate parts of Asia. The fruit is produced in very large quantities and exported in to northern countries; it is also pressed for oil and used for various domestic purposes. There are numerous varieties of this species, but the two chief kinds are the bitter almond and the sweet almond. The sweet almond affords a favorite article for dessert, but it contains little nourishment, and of all nuts is the most difficult of digestion. The tree has been cultivated in England for about three centuries for the sake of its beautiful foliage, as the fruit will not ripen without a greater degree of heat than is found in that climate. The distilled water of the bitter almond is highly injurious to the human species, and, taken in a large dose, produces almost instant death.' The prussic acid which can be obtained from the kernel of the peach is found also in the bitter almond."

"But what do they want to find it for," asked Malcolm, "when it kills people?"

"Because," replied his governess, "like some other noxious things, it can be made valuable when used moderately and in the right way. But it is often employed to give a flavor to intoxicating liquors, and this is not a right way, as it makes them even more dangerous than before. But we will leave the prussic acid and return to our almond tree. It flourishes in Palestine, where it blooms in January, and in March the ripe fruit can be gathered."

This seemed wonderfully strange to the children--flowers in January and fruit in March; and Miss Harson explained to them that in that part of the world they do not often have our bitter cold weather with its ice and snow to kill the tender buds.

"This tree," continued Miss Harson, "is occasionally mentioned in the Old Testament. In Jeremiah the prophet says, 'I see a rod of an almond tree[13];' also in Ecclesiastes it is said that 'the almond tree shall flourish[14].'"

[13] Jer. i. II.

[14] Eccl. xii. 5.

"Are there ever many peach trees growing in one place," asked Clara, "like the apple trees in Mr. Grove's orchard?"

"Yes," was the reply, "for in some places there are immense peach-orchards, covering many acres of ground; and when the trees in these are in blossom, the spring landscape seems to be pink with them. These great peach-fields are found in Delaware and Maryland, where the fruit grows in such perfection, and also in some of the Western States. We all know how delicious it is, but, unfortunately, so does a certain green worm, who curls up in the leaves which he gnaws in spite of the prussic acid. This insect will often attack the finest peaches and lay its eggs in them when the fruit is but half grown. In this way the young grubs find food and lodging provided for them all in one, and they thrive, while the peach decays."

"What a shame it is," exclaimed Malcolm, in great indignation, "to have our best peaches eaten by wretched little worms who might just as well eat grass and leave the peaches for us!"

"Perhaps they think it a shame that they are so often shaken to the ground or washed off the trees," replied Miss Harson; "and, as to their eating grass, they evidently prefer peaches. 'Insects as well as human beings have discriminating tastes, and the poor plum tree suffers even more than the peach from their attentions. In some parts of the country it has been entirely given up to their depredations, and farmers will not try to raise this fruit because of these active enemies. The whole almond family are liable to the attacks of insects. Canker-worms of one or of several species often strip them of their leaves; the tent-caterpillars pitch their tents among the branches and carry on their dangerous depredations; the slug-worms, the offspring of a fly called Selandria cerasi, reduce the leaves to skeletons, and thus destroy them; the cherry-weevils penetrate their bark, cover their branches with warts and cause them to decay; and borers gnaw galleries in their trunks and devour the inner bark and sap-wood.' So you see that, with such an army of destroyers, we may be thankful to get any fruit at all."

"I'm glad to know the name of that fly," said Malcolm, who considered it an additional grievance that it should have such a long name, "but I won't try to call him by it if I meet him anywhere."

"I think it's pretty," said Clara, beginning to repeat it, and making a decided failure.

"Fortunately," continued their governess, after reading it again for them, "there are other things much more important for you to remember just now, and I could not have said it myself without the book. And now let us see what else we can learn about the plum. It is a native, it seems, of North America, Europe and Asia, and many of the wild species are thorny. The cultivated plums, damsons and gages are varieties of the Prunus domestica, the cultivated plum tree. These have no thorns; the leaves are oval in shape, and the flowers grow singly. The most highly-valued cultivated plum trees came originally from the East, where they have been known from time immemorial. In many countries of Eastern Europe domestic animals are fattened on their fruits, and an alcoholic liquor is obtained from them; they also yield a white, crystallizable sugar. The prunes which we import from France are the dried fruit of varieties of the plum which contain a sufficient quantity of sugar to preserve the fruit from decay."

"Do prunes really grow on trees, Miss Harson?" asked Edith, who was rather disposed to think that they grew in pretty boxes.

"Yes, dear," was the reply; "they grow just as our plums do, only they are dried and packed in layers before they reach this country. We have two species of wild plum in North America--the beach-plum, a low shrub found in New England, the fruit of which is dark blue and about the size of damsons; while the other is quite a large tree, and very showy when covered with its scarlet fruit. In Maine it is called plum-granate, probably from its red color," "I know what's coming next," said Clara--"cherries; because all the rest have been used up. And then we're to have the story."

"But they're all interesting," replied Malcolm, gallantly, "because Miss Harson makes them so."

"I hope that is not the only reason," said his governess, laughing, "for trees are always beautiful and interesting and it is a privilege to be able to learn something of their habits and history.--Like most fruit trees, the cherry has many varieties, but it is always a handsome tree, and less spoiled by insects than others of the almond family. The black cherry is the most common species in the United States, and is both wild and cultivated. The garden cherry has broad, ovate, rough and serrate leaves, growing thickly on the branches, and this, with the height of the tree, makes a fine shade. Some old cherry trees have huge trunks, and their thick branches spread to a great distance. The branches of the wild cherry are too straggling to make a beautiful tree, and the leaves are small and narrow. The blossoms of the cultivated cherry are in umbels, while those of the wild cherry are borne in racemes."

"I remember that, Miss Harson," said Clara, pleased with her knowledge. "'Umbel' means 'like an umbrella,' and 'raceme' means 'growing along a stem.'"

"Very well indeed!" was the reply; "I am glad you have not forgotten it.--Of our cultivated cherries, we have here at Elmridge, besides the large black ones, which are so very sweet about the first of July, the great ox-hearts, which look like painted wax and ripen in June, and those very acid red ones, often called pie-cherries, which are used for pies and preserves. The cherry is a beautiful fruit, and one that is popular with birds as well as with boys. The great northern cherry of Europe, which was named by Linnaeus the 'bird-cherry,' is encouraged in Great Britain and on the Continent for the benefit of the birds, which are regarded as the most important checks to the over-multiplication of insects. The fact not yet properly understood in America--that the birds which are the most mischievous consumers of fruit are the most useful as destroyers of insects--is well known by all farmers in Europe; and while we destroy the birds to save the fruit, and sometimes cut down the fruit-trees to starve the birds, the Europeans more wisely plant them for the food and accommodation of the birds."

"Isn't it wicked to kill the poor little birds?" asked Edith.

"Yes, dear; it is cruel to kill them just for sport, as is often done, and very foolish, as we have just seen, to destroy them for the sake of the fruit, which the insects make way with in much greater quantities than the birds do."

"Miss Harson," asked Clara, "do people cut down real cherry trees to make the pretty red furniture like that in your room?"

"It is the wood of the wild cherry," replied her governess, "that is used for this purpose. It is of a light-red or fresh mahogany color, growing darker and richer with age. It is very close-grained, compact, takes a good polish, and when perfectly seasoned is not liable to shrink or warp. It is therefore particularly suitable, and much employed, for tables, chests of drawers, and other cabinet-work, and when polished and varnished is not less beautiful for such articles than are inferior kinds of mahogany."

"'Cherry' sounds pretty to say," continued Clara. "I wonder how the tree got that name?"

"That wonder is easily explained," said Miss Harson, "for I have been reading about it, and I was just going to tell you. 'Cherry comes from 'Cerasus,' the name of a town on the Black Sea from whence the tree is supposed to have been introduced into Italy, and it designates a genus of about forty species, natives of all the temperate regions of the northern hemisphere. They are trees or shrubs with smooth serrated leaves, which are folded together when young, and white or reddish flowers growing in bunches, like umbels, and preceding the leaves or in terminal racemes accompanying or following the leaves. A few species, with numerous varieties, produce valuable fruits; nearly all are remarkable for the abundance of their early flowers, sometimes rendered double by cultivation. And now," added the young lady, "we have arrived at the story, which is translated from the German; and in Germany the cherries are particularly fine. A plateful of this beautiful fruit was, as you will see, the cause of some remarkable changes."

CHAPTER XI.

THE CHERRY-STORY.

On the banks of the Rhine, in the pleasant little village of Rebenheim, lived Ehrenberg, the village mayor. He was much respected for his virtues, and his wife was greatly beloved for her charity to the poor. They had an only daughter--the little Caroline--who gave early promise of a superior mind and a benevolent heart. She was the idol of her parents, who devoted their whole care to giving her a sound religious education.

Not far from the house, and close to the orchard and kitchen-garden, there was another little garden, planted exclusively with flowers. The day that Caroline was born her father planted a cherry tree in the middle of the flower-garden. He had chosen a tree with a short trunk, in order that his little daughter could more easily admire the blossoms and pluck the cherries when they were ripe.

When the tree bloomed for the first time and was so covered with blossoms that it looked like a single bunch of white flowers, the father and mother came out one morning to enjoy the sight. Little Caroline was in her mother's arms. The infant smiled, and, stretching out her little hands for the blossoms, endeavored at the same time to speak her joy, but in such a way as no one but a mother could understand:

"Flowers! flowers! Pretty! pretty!"

The child engaged more of the parents' thoughts than all the cherry-blossoms and gardens and orchards, and all they were worth. They resolved to educate her well; they prayed to God to bless their care and attention by making Caroline worthy of him and the joy and consolation of her parents. As soon as the little girl was old enough to understand, her mother told her lovingly of that kind Father in heaven who makes the flowers bloom and the trees bud and the cherries and apples grow ruddy and ripe; she told her also of the blessed Son of God, once an infant like herself, who died for all the world.

The cherry tree in the middle of the garden was given to Caroline for her own, and it was a greater treasure to her than were all the flowers. She watched and admired it every day, from the moment the first bud appeared until the cherries were ripe. She grieved when she saw the white blossoms turn yellow and drop to the earth, but her grief was changed into joy when the cherries appeared, green at first and smaller than peas, and then daily growing larger and larger, until the rich red skin of the ripe cherry at last blushed among the interstices of the green leaves.

"Thus it is," said her father; "youth and beauty fade like the blossoms, but virtue is the fruit which we expect from the tree. This whole world is, as it were, a large garden, in which God has appointed to every man a place, that he may bring forth abundant and good fruit. As God sends rain and sunshine on the trees, so does he send down grace on men to make them grow in virtue, if they will but do their part."

In the course of time war approached the quiet village which had hitherto been the abode of peace and domestic bliss, and the battle raged fearfully. Balls and shells whizzed about, and several houses caught fire. As soon as the danger would permit, the mayor tried to extinguish the flames, while his wife and little daughter were praying earnestly for themselves and for their neighbors.

In the afternoon a ring was heard at the door, and, looking out of the window, Madame Ehrenberg saw an officer of hussars standing before her. Fortunately, he was a German, and mother and daughter ran to open the door.

"Do not be alarmed," said the officer, in a friendly tone, when he saw the frightened faces; "the danger is over, and you are quite safe. The fire in the village, too, is almost quenched, and the mayor will soon be here. I beg you for some refreshment, if it is only a morsel of bread and a drink of water. It was sharp work," he added, wiping the perspiration from his brow, "but, thank God, we have conquered," Provisions were scarce, for the village had been plundered by the enemy, but the good lady brought forth a flask of wine and some rye bread, with many regrets that she had nothing better to offer. But the visitor, as he ate the bread with a hearty relish, declared that it was enough, for it was the first morsel he had tasted that day.

Caroline ran and brought in on a porcelain plate some of the ripest cherries from her own tree.

"Cherries!" exclaimed the officer. "They are a rarity in this district. How did they escape the enemy? All the trees in the country around are stripped."

"The cherries," said the mother, "are from a little tree which was planted in Caroline's flower-garden on her birthday. It is but a few days since they became ripe; the enemy, perhaps, did not notice the little tree."

"And is it for me you intend the cherries, my dear child?" asked the officer. "Oh no; you must keep them. It were a pity to take one of them from you."

"How could we refuse a few cherries," said Caroline, "to the man that sheds his blood in our defence? You must eat them all," said she, while the tears streamed down her cheeks. "Do, I entreat you! Eat them all."

He took some of the cherries and laid them on the table, near his wine-glass; but he had scarcely placed the glass to his lips when the trumpet sounded. He sprang up and girded on his sword.

"That is the signal to march," said he. "I cannot wait one instant."

Caroline wrapped the cherries in a roll of white paper and insisted that he should put them in his pocket.

"The weather is very warm," said she, "and even cherries will be some refreshment."

"Oh," said the officer, with emotion, "what a happiness it is for a soldier, who is often obliged to snatch each morsel from unwilling hands, to meet with a generous and benevolent family! I wish it were in my power, my dear child, to give you some pledge of my gratitude, but I have nothing--not so much as a single groat. You must be content with my simple thanks." With these words, and once more bidding Caroline and her mother an affectionate farewell, he took his departure, and walked rapidly out of sight.

The joy of the good family for their happy deliverance was, alas! of short continuance. Some weeks after, a dreadful battle was fought near the village, which was reduced to a heap of ruins. The mayor's house was burned to the ground and all his property destroyed. Alas for the horrors of cruel war! Father, mother and daughter fled away on foot, and wept bitterly when they looked back on their once happy village, now but a mass of blazing ruins.

The family retired to a distant town, and lived there in very great distress. The mayor endeavored to obtain a livelihood as a scrivener, or clerk; his wife worked at dressmaking and millinery, and Caroline, who soon became skillful in such matters, faithfully assisted her.

A lady in town--the Countess von Buchenhaim--gave them much employment, and one day Caroline went to this lady's house to carry home a bonnet. She was taken to the garden, where the countess was sitting in the summer-house with her sister and nieces, who had come to visit her. The young ladies were delighted with the bonnet, and their mother gave orders for three more, particularly praising the blue flowers, which were the work of Caroline's own hands.

The Countess von Buchenhaim spoke very kindly of the young girl to her sister, and related the sad story of the worthy family's misfortunes. The count was standing with his brother-in-law, the colonel, at some little distance from the door of the summer-house, and the colonel, a fine-looking man in a hussar's uniform and with a star on his breast, overheard the conversation. Coming up, he looked closely at Caroline.

"Is it possible," said he, "that you are the daughter of the mayor of Rebenheim? How tall you have grown! I should scarcely have recognized you, though we are old acquaintances."

Caroline stood there abashed, looking full in the face of the stranger, her cheeks covered with blushes. Taking her by the hand, the colonel conducted her to his wife, who was sitting near the countess.

"See, Amelia," said he; "this is the young lady who saved my life ten years ago, when she was only a child."

"How can that be possible?" asked Caroline, in amazement.

"It must indeed appear incomprehensible to you," answered the colonel, "but do you remember the hussar-officer that one day, after a battle, stood knocking at the door of your father's house in Rebenheim? Do you remember the cherries which you so kindly gave him?"

"Oh, was it you?" exclaimed Caroline, while her face beamed with a smile of recognition. "Thank God you are alive! But how I could have done anything toward saving your life I cannot understand."

"In truth, it would be impossible for you to guess the great service you did me," said he, "but my wife and daughters know it well; I wrote to them of it at once. And I look upon it as one of the most remarkable occurrences of my life."

"And one that I ought to remember better than any other event of the war," said his lady, rising and affectionately embracing Caroline.

"Well," said the countess, "neither I nor my husband ever heard the story. Please give us a full account of it."

"Oh, it is easily told," said the colonel. "Hungry and thirsty, I entered the house in which Caroline and her parents dwelt, and, to tell the plain truth, I begged for some bread and water. They gave me a share of the best they had, and did not hesitate to do so, though their village and themselves were in the greatest distress. Caroline robbed every bough on her cherry tree to refresh me. Fine cherries they were--the only ones, probably, in the whole country. But the enemy did not give me time to eat them; I was obliged to depart in a hurry. Caroline insisted, with the kindest hospitality, that I should take them with me, but that was no easy matter: my horse had been shot under me the day before. I took from my knapsack whatever articles I could in a hurry, and, thrusting them into my pockets, I fought on foot until a hussar gave me his horse. All that I was worth was in my pockets, so that to make room for the cherries I was obliged to take the pocket-book out of my pocket and place it here beneath my vest. The enemy, who had been driven back, made a feint of advancing on us, and I led down my hussars in gallant style. But suddenly we found ourselves in front of a body of infantry concealed behind a hedge. One of them fired at me, and the fellow had taken good aim, for the ball struck me here on the breast. But it rebounded from the pocket-book; otherwise, I should have been shot through the body and fallen dead on the spot. Tell me," said he, in a tone of deep emotion; "was not that little child an instrument in the hand of God to save me from death? Am I right or not when I give Caroline the credit, under God, of having saved my life? Her must I thank that my Amelia is not a widow and my daughters orphans."

All agreed with him. His wife, who had Caroline's hand locked in her own during the whole narrative, now pressed it affectionately and with tears in her eyes.

"You, then," said she, "were the good angel that averted such a terrible misfortune from our family?"

Her two daughters also gazed with pleasure at Caroline.

"Every time we ate cherries," said the younger, "we spoke of you without knowing you."

All had kind and grateful words for the young girl, but the colonel soon bade her farewell for the present, and said that he had some business to attend to with his brother-in-law. This business was to urge the count to appoint Ehrenberg his steward in place of the one who had died a few months before. A better man, he said, could not be found; for when he had visited Rebenheim to make inquiries for the family, although none could tell where they had gone, all were loud in their praise, and the mayor was pronounced a pattern of justice, honor and charity.

The count drew out the order, signed it, and gave it to his brother-in-law, who wished himself to take it to Mr. Ehrenberg; and he went at once to the house and saluted him as "master-steward of Buchenhaim."

"Read that," he said to the astonished man as he handed him the paper in which he was duly appointed steward of Buchenhaim, with a good salary of a thousand thalers and several valuable perquisites.

"And you," said the colonel to Caroline and her mother, "must prepare to remove at once. Your lodgings are so confined! But you will find it very different in the house which you are to occupy in Buchenhaim. The dwelling is large and commodious, with a fine garden attached, well stocked with cherry trees. Next Monday you will be there, and this very day you must start. What a happy feast we shall have there!--not like the hasty meal you gave the hussar-officer amid the thunder of cannon and the blazing roofs of Rebenheim. Do not forget to have cherries, dear Caroline, for dessert; I think they will be fully ripe by that time."

With these words the colonel hurried away to escape the thanks of this good family, and, in truth, to conceal his own tears. So rapidly did he disappear that Ehrenberg could scarcely accompany him down the steps.

"Oh, Caroline," said the happy father when he returned, "who could have imagined that the little cherry tree I planted in the flower-garden the day you were born would ever produce such good fruit?"

"It was the providence of God," exclaimed the mother, clasping her hands. "I remember distinctly the first time the blossoms appeared on that tree, when you and I went out to look at it, and little Caroline, then an infant in my arms, was so much delighted with the white flowers. We resolved then to educate our daughter piously, and prayed fervently to God that she, who was then as full of promise as the blossoms on the tree, might by his grace one day be the prop of our old age. That prayer is now fulfilled beyond our fondest anticipations. Praise for ever be to the name of God!"

Edith declared that this was one of the very sweetest stories Miss Harson had ever told them, and Clara and Malcolm were equally well pleased with it.

"Were those cherries like ours?" asked Clara.

"They were larger and finer than ours generally are, I think," was the reply, "being the great northern cherry, or bird-cherry, of Europe, which grows in Germany to great perfection. And the little German girl's plate of cherries, which she so generously urged upon a stranger when food of any kind was so scarce, is a beautiful illustration of the first verse of the eleventh chapter of Proverbs: 'Cast thy bread upon the waters; for thou shalt find it after many days.'"

CHAPTER XII.

THE MULBERRY FAMILY.

"There is a fruit tree," said Miss Harson, "belonging to an entirely different family, which we have not considered yet; and, although it is not a common tree with us, one specimen of it is to be found in Mrs. Bush's garden, where you have all enjoyed the fruit very much. What is it?"

"Mulberry," said Clara, promptly, while Malcolm was wondering what it could be.

"Oh yes," said Edith, very innocently; "I like to go and see Mrs. Bush when there are mulberries."

Mrs. Bush was not a cheerful person to visit, as she was quite old and rather hard of hearing, and she lived alone in the gloomy old house with the Lombardy poplars in front, where everything looked dark and shut up. A queer woman in a sunbonnet, nearly as old as Mrs. Bush, lived close by, and "kept an eye on her," as she said.

Mrs. Bush's great enjoyment was to have visitors of all ages, to whom she talked a great deal, and cried as she talked, about a daughter who had died a few years ago. The little Kyles did not care to go there except when, as Edith said, there were ripe mulberries; but Mrs. Bush liked very much to have them, and Miss Harson took her little charges there occasionally, because, as she explained to them, it gave pleasure to a lonely old woman, and such visits were just as much charity, though of a different kind, as giving food and clothes to those who need them. The children delighted in the mulberries just because they did not have them at home, although they had fruit that was very much nicer; but Miss Harson never wished even to taste them, although she too had liked them when a little girl.

"The mulberry tree," continued their governess, "belongs to the bread-fruit family, but the other members of this remarkable family, except the Osage orange, are found only in foreign countries. The bread-fruit tree itself, the fig, the Indian fig, or banyan tree, and the deadly upas tree, are all relations of the mulberry."

"Well, trees are queer things," exclaimed Malcolm, "to belong to families that are not a bit alike."

"They are alike in important points, when we examine them carefully," was the reply. "The bread-fruit genus consists, with a single exception, of trees and shrubs with alternate, toothed or lobed or entire leaves and milky juice. This reminds me that the famous cow tree of South America, which yields a large supply of rich and wholesome milk, is one of the members; and you see what a number of famous trees we have on hand now. There are several kinds of mulberries--the red, black, white and paper mulberry, which are all occasionally found in this country, and they were once quite popular here for their shade. The fruit is unusually small for tree-fruit, and very soft when ripe, as you all know; it is not unlike a long, narrow blackberry, and forms, like it, a compound fruit, as though many small berries had grown together. The tree in Mrs. Bush's garden is the black mulberry, as any one might know by the stained lips and hands that sometimes come from there; and it has been cultivated from ancient times for its fine appearance and shade. It is found wild in the forests of Persia, and is thought to have been taken from there to Europe. The tree is more beautiful than useful, for the silkworms do not thrive well on the leaves and the wood is neither strong nor durable."

"Why, I thought," said Clara, "that silkworms always lived on mulberry-leaves?"

"The white mulberry is their favorite food; and another species, called the Morus multicaulis--for Morus is the scientific name of the family--has more delicate leaves than any other, and produces a finer quality of silk. These trees are natives of China, and the white mulberry grows very rapidly to the height of thirty or forty feet. The paper mulberry is so called because in China and Japan--of which it is a native--its bark is manufactured into paper. In the South-Sea Islands, where it is also found, the bark is made into the curious dresses which we sometimes see imported thence. It is a low, thick-branched tree with large light-colored downy leaves and dark-scarlet fruit."

"I wonder," said Malcolm, "if the bark is like birch-bark?"

"It does not look like it," replied Miss Harson, "but it seems to be very much of the same nature. The red mulberry and black mulberry are the most hardy of these trees, and the red mulberry will thrive farther north than any of the family. The wood is valuable for many purposes for which timber is used, and especially in boat-building. And now, as we learned something about silkworms and their cocoons in our talks about insects[15], there is little more to be said of the mulberry tree which any but learned people would care to know."

[15] See Flyers and Crawlers. Presbyterian Board of Publication.

"I want to hear about the bread tree," said little Edith, "and how the loaves of bread grow on it."

"Do they, Miss Harson?" asked Clara, not exactly seeing how this could be.

"I don't believe they're very hot," remarked Malcolm, who was puzzled over the bread-fruit tree himself, but who laughed at his little sister's idea in a very knowing way. It was not an ill-natured laugh, though, and a glance from his governess always quieted him.

"No, dear," replied Miss Harson, answering Clara; "loaves of bread do not grow on any tree. But I will tell you about the bread-fruit presently; let us finish the Morus family and their kindred in our own country before we go to their foreign relations. The Osage orange is so much used in the United States, and in this part of it, for hedges, on account of its rapid growth and ornamental appearance, that we really ought to know something about it. 'It is a beautiful low, spreading, round-headed tree with the port and splendor of an orange tree. Its oval, entire, polished leaves have the shining green of natives of warmer regions, and its curiously-tesselated, succulent compound fruit the size and golden color of an orange. It was first found in the country of the Osage Indians, from whom it gets its name, and it has since been cultivated in many parts of this country and in Europe. The Osages belonged to the Sioux, or Dacotah, tribe of Indians, and their home was in the south-western part of the old United States. The Osage orange--a tree from thirty to forty feet high with leaves even more bright and glossy than those of the ordinary orange--was first found growing wild near one of their villages."

"But what a very high hedge it would make!" said Malcolm.

"Yes, if left to its natural growth, it would be a very absurd fence indeed. But this is not the case; the branches spread out very widely, and by cutting off the tops and trimming the remainder twice in a season a very handsome thickset hedge is produced, with lustrous leaves and sharp, straight thorns. Another name for this tree is yellow-wood, or bow-wood, because the wood is of a bright-yellow color, and the grain is so fine and elastic that the Southern Indians have been in the habit of using it to make their bows. The experiment of feeding silkworms upon the leaves has been tried, but it was not very successful."

"I suppose the worms didn't know that it belonged to the mulberry family," said Clara, "and I don't see now why it does."

For reply, her governess read:

"'The sap of the young wood and of the leaves is milky and contains a large proportion of caoutchouc.'"

"Oh!" exclaimed Malcolm; "that sounds just like sneezing. What is it, Miss Harson?"

"Something that you wear on your feet and over your shoulders in wet weather; so now guess."

"Overshoes!" replied Clara, in a great hurry.

"How many of them do you wear over your shoulders at once?" asked her brother. "And it must be a queer kind of sap that has overshoes in it. Why couldn't you say 'India-rubber'?"

"And why couldn't you say it before Clara put it into your head by saying 'Overshoes?" asked Miss Harson. "Clara has the right idea, only she did not express it in the clearest way. The sap of the caoutchouc, or India-rubber, tree is the most valuable yet discovered, and, as it is of a milky nature, it can very properly be brought into the present class of trees."

"Is that a mulberry too?" asked Clara, who thought that the size of the family was getting beyond all bounds.

"It is not really set down as belonging to the bread-fruit family," was the reply, "but it certainly has the peculiarity of their milky sap. However, as I know that you are all eager to hear about the bread-fruit tree, we will take that next. This tree is found in various tropical regions, but principally in the South-Sea Islands, where it is about forty feet high. The immense leaves are half a yard long and over a quarter wide, and are deeply divided into sharp lobes. The fruit looks like a very large green berry, being about the size of a cocoanut or melon, and the proper time for gathering it is about a week before it is ripe. When baked, it is not very unlike bread. It is cooked by being cut into several pieces, which are baked in an oven in the ground. It is often eaten with orange-juice and cocoanut-milk. Some of the South-Sea islanders depend very much upon it for their food. The large seeds, when roasted, are said to taste like the best chestnuts. The pulp, which is the bread-part, is said to resemble a baked potato and is very white and tender, but, unless eaten soon after the fruit is gathered, it grows hard and choky."

"So Edie's 'loaves of bread' are green?" said Malcolm, rather teasingly.

"That's because they grow on a tree," replied Clara. "Our loaves of bread are raw dough before they're baked, and they are grains of wheat before they are dough."

"That is quite true, dear," replied her governess, laughing, "and we must teach Malcolm not to be quite so critical.--The bread-fruit is a wonderful tree, and it certainly does bear uncooked loaves of bread, at least, for they require no kneading to be ready for the oven. The fruit is to be found on the tree for eight months of the year--which is very different from any of our fruits--and two or three bread-fruit trees will supply one man with food all the year round."

"Put what does he do when there is no fresh fruit on them?" asked Malcolm. "You told us that it was not good to eat unless it was fresh."

"We should not think it good, but the native makes it into a sour paste called mah? and the people of the islands eat this during the four months when the fresh fruit is not to be had. The bread-fruit is said to be very nourishing, and it can be prepared in various ways. The timber of this tree, though soft, is found useful in building houses and boats; the flowers, when dried, serve for tinder; the viscid, milky juice answers for birdlime and glue; the leaves, for towels and packing; and the inner bark, beaten together, makes one species of the South-Sea cloth."

"What a very useful tree!" exclaimed Clara.

"It is indeed," replied Miss Harson; "and this is the case with many of the trees found in these warm countries, where the inhabitants know little of the arts and manufactures, and would almost starve rather than exert themselves very greatly. There is another species of bread-fruit, called the jaca, or jack, tree, found on the mainland of Asia, which produces its fruit on different parts of the tree, according to its age. When the tree is young, the fruit grows from the twigs; in middle age it grows from the trunk; and when the tree gets old, it grows from the roots."

There was a picture of the jack tree with fruit growing out of the trunk and great branches like melons, and the children crowded eagerly around to look at it. All agreed that it was the very queerest tree they had yet heard of.

"The fruit is even larger than that of the island bread-fruit," continued their governess, "but it is not so pleasant to our taste, nor is it so nourishing. It often weighs over thirty pounds and has two or three hundred seeds, each of which is four times as large as an almond and is surrounded by a pulp which is greatly relished by the natives of India. The seeds, or nuts, are roasted, like those of smaller fruit, and make very good chestnuts. The fruit has a strong odor not very agreeable to noses not educated to it."

"Miss Harson," said Malcolm, "what is the upas tree like, and why is it called deadly?"

"It is a tree eighty feet high, with white and slightly-furrowed bark; the branches, which are very thick, grow nearly at the top, dividing into smaller ones, which form an irregular sort of crown to the tall, straight trunk. There is no reason for calling it deadly except a foolish notion and the fact that a very strong poison is prepared from the milky sap. The tree grows in the island of Java, and for a long time many fabulous stories were told of its dangerous nature. Travelers in that region would send home the wildest and most improbable stories of the poison tree, until the very name of the upas was enough to make people shudder. It is said that a Dutch surgeon stationed on the island did much to keep up the impression. He wrote an account of the valley in which the upas was said to be growing alone, for no tree nor shrub was to be found near it. And he declared that neither animal nor bird could breathe the noxious effluvia from the tree without instant death. In fact, he called this fatal spot 'The Valley of Death.'"

"And wasn't it true, Miss Harson?"

"Not all true, Clara; some one who had spent many years in Java proved these stories to be entirely false. Instead of growing in a dismal valley by itself, the graceful-looking upas tree is found in the most fertile spots, among other trees, and very often climbing plants are twisted round its trunk, while birds nestle in the branches. It can be handled, too, like any other tree; and all this is as unlike the Dutch surgeon's account as possible. One of his stories was that the criminals on the island were employed to collect the poison from the trunk of the tree; that they were permitted to choose whether to die by the hand of the executioner or to go to the upas for a box of its fatal juice; and that the ground all about the tree was strewed with the dead bodies of those who had perished on this errand."

"Oh," exclaimed Edith, "wasn't that dreadful?"

"The story was dreadful, dear, but it was only a story, you know: the upas tree did not kill people at all; and to turn the milky juice into a dangerous poison took a great deal of time and trouble. It was mixed with various spices and fermented; when ready for use, it was poured into the hollow joints of bamboo and carefully kept from the air. Both for war and for the chase arrows are dipped in this fatal preparation, and the effect has been witnessed by naturalists on animals, and also on man. The instant it touches the blood it is carried through the whole system, so that it may be felt in all the veins and causes a burning sensation, especially in the head, which is followed by sickness and death."

"Well," said Clara, drawing a long breath, "I'm glad that I don't live in Java."

"The poisoned arrows are not constantly flying about in Java, dear," replied her governess, with a smile, "and I do not think you would be in any danger from them; but there are a great many other reasons why it is not pleasant, except for natives, to live in Java. There are a number of Dutch settlers there, because the island was conquered by the Dutch nation, but while war with the natives was going on they suffered terribly from these poisoned arrows; so that the very name of upas caused them to tremble. The word 'upas,' in the language of the natives, means poison, and there is in the island a valley called the upas, or poison, valley. It has nothing, however, to do with the tree, which does not grow anywhere in the neighborhood. That valley may literally be called 'The Valley of Death.' We are told that it came to exist in this way: The largest mountain in Java was once partly buried in a very dreadful manner. In the middle of a summer night the people in the neighborhood perceived a luminous cloud that seemed wholly to envelop the mountain.

They were extremely alarmed and took to flight, but ere they could escape a terrific noise was heard, like the discharge of cannon, and part of the mountain fell in and disappeared. At the same moment quantities of stones and lava were thrown to the distance of several miles. Fifteen miles of ground covered with villages and plantations were swallowed up or buried under the lava from the mountain; and when all was over and people tried to visit the scene of the disaster, they could not approach it on account of the heat of the stones and other substances piled upon one another. And yet as much as six weeks had elapsed since the catastrophe. This upas valley is about half a mile in circumference, and the vapor that escapes through the cracks and fissures is fatal to every living thing. Here, indeed, are to be seen the bones of animals and birds, and even the skeletons of human beings who were unfortunate enough to enter and were overpowered by the deadly vapor. And now," added Miss Harson, "I have given you this account to make you understand that the famous upas valley of Java is not a valley of upas trees, but one of poisonous vapors."

"And the deadly upas," said Malcolm, "is not deadly, after all! I think I shall remember that."

"And I too," said Clara and Edith, who had listened with great interest to the description.

"Shall we have some figs now, by way of variety?" was a question that caused three pairs of eyes to turn rather expectantly on the speaker; for figs were very popular with the small people of Elmridge.

"Not in the way of refreshments, just at present," continued their governess, "but only as belonging to the mulberry family; and we will begin with that curious tree the banyan, or Indian fig. This stately and beautiful tree is found on the banks of the river Ganges and in many parts of India, and is a tree much valued and venerated by the Hindu. He plants it near the temple of his idol; and if the village in which he resides does not possess any such edifice, he uses the banyan for a temple and places the idol beneath it. Here, every morning and evening, he performs the rites of his heathen worship. And, more than this, he considers the tree, with its out-stretched and far-sheltering arms, an emblem of the creator of all things."

"Is that only one tree?" asked Malcolm as Miss Harson displayed a picture that was more like a small grove. "Why, it looks like two or three trees together."

"Does it grow up from the ground or down from the air?" asked Clara. "Just look at these queer branches with one end fast to the tree and the other end fast to the ground!"

Edith thought that the branches which had not reached the ground looked like snakes, but, for all that, it was certainly a grand tree.

"The peculiar growth of the banyan," continued Miss Harson, "renders it an object of beauty and produces those column-like stems that cause it to become a grove in itself. It may be said to grow, not from the seed, but from the branches. They spread out horizontally, and each branch sends out a number of rootlets that at first hang from it like slender cords and wave about in the wind.--Those are your 'snakes,' Edith.--But by degrees they reach the ground and root themselves into it; then the cord tightens and thickens and becomes a stem, acting like a prop to the widespreading branch of the parent plant. Indeed, column on column is added in this manner, the books tell us, so long as the mother-tree can support its numerous progeny."

"How very strange!" said Clara. "The mulberry seems to have some very funny relations."

"Such a great tree ought to bear very large figs," added Malcolm.

"On the contrary," replied his governess, "it bears uncommonly small ones--no larger than a hazel-nut, and of a red color. They are not considered eatable by the natives, but birds and animals feed upon them, and in the leafy bower of the banyan are found the peacock, the monkey and the squirrel. Here, too, are a myriad of pigeons as green as the leaf and with eyes and feet of a brilliant red. They are so like the foliage in color that they can be seen only by the practiced eye of the hunter, and even he would fail to detect them were it not for their restless movements. As they flutter about from branch to branch they are apt to fall victims to his skill in shooting his arrows."

"If they would only keep still!" exclaimed Edith, who felt a strong sympathy for the green pigeons. "Poor pretty things! Why don't they, Miss Harson, instead of getting killed?"

"They do not know their danger until it is too late, and it is quite as hard for them to keep still as it is for little girls."

Edith wondered if that meant her; she was a little girl, but she did not think she was so very restless. However, Miss Harson didn't tell her, and she soon forgot it in listening to what was said of the queer tree with branches like snakes.

"The leaves of the banyan tree are large and soft and of a very bright green, and the deep shade and pillared walks are so welcome to the Hindu that he even tries to improve on Nature and coax the shoots to grow just where he wishes them. He binds wet clay and moss on the branch to make the rootlet sprout."

"Will it grow then?" asked Malcolm.

"Yes, just as a cutting planted in the earth will grow, although it seems a very odd style of gardening.--The sacred fig tree of India--Ficus religiosa--is a near relative of the banyan, and very much like it in general appearance; but the leaves are on such slender stalks that they tremble like those of the aspen. It is known as the bo tree of Ceylon, and is said to have been placed in charge of the priests long before the present race of inhabitants had appeared in the island."

"Where do the real figs grow?" asked Clara.

"In a great many moderately warm or sub-tropical countries," was the reply, "but Smyrna figs are the most celebrated. Immense quantities of the fruit are dried and packed in Asiatic Turkey for exportation from this city, and it is said that in the fig season nothing else is talked about there."

"I didn't know that they were dried," said Malcolm, in great surprise; "I thought they were just packed tight in boxes and then sent off."

"'In its native country,'" read Miss Harson, "'and when growing on the tree, the fig presents a different appearance from the dried and packed specimens we see in this country. It is a firm and fleshy fruit, and has a delicious honey-drop hanging from the point.' And here," she added, "is a small branch from the fig tree, with fruit growing on it."

"Why, it's shaped like a pear!" exclaimed Malcolm.

"And what large, pretty leaves it has!" said Clara.

"'The fig tree is common in Palestine and the East,'" Miss Harson continued to read, "'and flourishes with the greatest luxuriance in those barren and stony situations, where little else will grow. Its large size and its abundance of five-lobed leaves render it a pleasant shade-tree, and its fruit furnishes a wholesome food very much used in all the lands of the Bible.' Figs were among the fruits mentioned in the 'land that flowed with milk and honey,' and it was a symbol of peace and plenty, as you will find, Malcolm, by reading to us from First Kings, fourth chapter, twenty-fifth verse."

"'And Judah and Israel dwelt safely, every man under his vine and under his fig tree, from Dan even to Beersheba, all the days of Solomon.'--That's what it means, then!" said Malcolm, when he had finished reading the verse. "I've heard people say, 'Under your own vine and fig tree,' and I couldn't tell what they meant."

"Yes," replied his governess, "some persons make very free with the words of Holy Scripture and twist them to suit meanings for which they were not intended. Having a house of one's own is usually meant by this quotation, and almost the same words are repeated in other parts of the Old Testament. The fig is often mentioned in the Bible, and two kinds are spoken of--the very early fig, and the one that ripens late in the summer. The early fig was considered the best; and I think that Clara will tell us what is said of it by the prophet Jeremiah."

Clara read slowly:

"'One basket had very good figs, even like the figs that are first ripe; and the other basket had very naughty figs, which could not be eaten, they were so bad[16].'"

[16] Jer. xxiv. 2.

"But can figs be naughty, Miss Harson?" asked Edith, with very wide-open eyes. "I thought that only children were naughty,"

"There are 'naughty' grown people as well as naughty children," was the reply, "and inanimate things like figs in old times were called naughty too, in the sense of being bad.--The fruit of the fig tree appears not only before the leaves, but without any sign of blossoms, the flowers being small and hidden in the little buttons which first shoot out from the points of the sterns, and around which the outer and firm part of the fig grows. The leaves come out so late in the season that our Saviour said, 'Now learn a parable of the fig tree; when his branch is yet tender, and putteth forth leaves, ye know that summer is nigh[17].' Did not our Lord say something else about a fig tree?"

[17] Matt. xxiv. 32.

"Yes," replied Clara; "the one that was withered away because it had no figs on it."

"The barren fig tree which was withered at our Saviour's word, as an awful warning to unfruitful professors of religion, seems to have spent itself in leaves. It stood by the wayside, free to all, and, as the time for stripping the trees of their fruit had not come--for in Mark we are told that 'the time of figs was not yet[18]'--it was reasonable to expect to find it covered with figs in various stages of growth. Yet there was 'nothing thereon, but leaves only.' Find the nineteenth verse of the twenty-first chapter of Matthew, Malcolm, and read what is said there."

[18] Mark xi. 13.

"'And when he saw a fig tree in the way, he came to it, and found nothing thereon, but leaves only, and said unto it, Let no fruit grow on thee henceforward for ever. And presently the fig tree withered away.'"

"A fig tree having leaves," said Miss Harson, "should also have figs, for these, as I have already told you, appear before the leaves, and both are on the tree at the same time; so that, although unripe figs are seen without leaves, leaves should not be seen without figs; and if it was not yet the season for figs, it was not the season for leaves either. The barren fig tree has often been compared to people who make a show of goodness in words, but leave the doing of good works to others; and when anything is expected of them, there is sure to be disappointment. 'Nothing but leaves' has become a proverb; and when it can be used to express the barren condition of those who profess to follow the teachings of our Lord, it is sad indeed."

"Do fig trees grow wild?" asked Clara, presently.

"Yes," was the reply, "and very curious-looking things they are. 'Their roots twist into all kinds of whimsical contortions, so as to look more like a mass of snakes than the roots of a tree. They unite themselves so closely to the substances that come in their way, such as the face of rocks, or even the stems of other trees, that nothing can pull them away. And in some parts of India these strong, tough roots are made to serve the purpose of bridges and twisted over some stream or cataract. The wild fig is often a dangerous parasite, and does not attain perfection without completing some work of destruction among its neighbors in the forest. A slender rootlet may sometimes be seen hanging from the crown of a palm. The seed was carried there by some bird that had fed upon the fruit of a wild fig, and it rooted itself with surprising facility. The rootlet, as it descends, envelops the column-like stem of the palm with a woody network, and at length reaches the ground. Meanwhile, the true stem of the parasite shoots upward from the crown of the palm. It sends out numberless rootlets, each of which, as soon as it reaches the ground, takes root; and between them the palm is stifled and perishes, leaving the fig in undisturbed possession. The parasite does not, however, long survive the decline; for, no longer fed by the juices of the palm, it also, in process of time, begins to languish and decline.'"

"What a mean thing it is!" exclaimed Malcolm--"as mean as the cuckoo, that lays its eggs in other birds' nests. And I'm glad it dies when it has killed the palm tree; it just serves it right. But don't figs ever grow in this country, Miss Harson?"

"Yes," replied his governess; "they are cultivated in the Southern States and in California, like many other semi-tropical fruits, and are principally eaten fresh, but for drying they are not equal to the imported ones. No doubt the cultivation of figs in California will become a prosperous trade, for the climate and circumstances there are much like those of Syria."

CHAPTER XIII.

QUEER RELATIONS: THE CAOUTCHOUC AND THE MILK TREE.

"What dark, strange-looking trees!" exclaimed the children while looking at an illustration of caoutchouc trees in Brazil. "How thick and strong they are! And what funny tops!--like pointed umbrellas."

"The India-rubber tree is not likely to be mistaken for any other," said their governess, "and it does not look very dark and gloomy in that forest, where everything seems to be crowded close and in a tangle, because South American vegetation grows so thickly and rapidly. This is the country which supplies the largest quantity of India-rubber. Immense cargoes are shipped from the town of Para, on the river Amazon, and obtained from the Siphonia elastica."

"Are the stems all made of India-rubber?" asked Edith, who thought that was exactly what they looked like.

"Are the stems of the maple trees made of maple-sugar?" replied Miss Harson. "The India-rubber is got from its tree as the sugar is from the maple tree. It is taken from the trunk in the shape of a very thick milky fluid, and it is said that no other vital fluid, whether in animal or in plant, contains so much solid material within it; and it is a matter of surprise that the sap, thus encumbered, can circulate through all the delicate vessels of the tree. Tropical heat is required to form the caoutchouc; for when the tree is cultivated in hothouses, the substance of the sap is quite different. The full-grown trees are very handsome, with round column-like trunks about sixty feet high, and the crown of foliage is said to resemble that of the ash."

"Did people always know about India-rubber?" asked Clara.

"No indeed! It is not more than a hundred and fifty years--perhaps not so long--since it was a great curiosity; so that a piece half an inch square would sell in London for nearly a dollar of our money, but now it comes in shiploads, and a pound of it costs less than quarter of that sum. It is used for so many purposes that it seems as if the world could never have gone on without it. All sorts of outside garments to keep out the rain are made of it. Waterproof cloaks are called macintoshes in England because this was the name of the person who invented them. India-rubber is also used for tents and many other things, and, as water cannot get through it, there is a great saving of trouble and expense."

"It must be splendid for tents," said Malcolm; "no one need care, when snug under cover, whether or not it rained in the woods."

"People do care, though," was the reply, "for they expect, when in the woods, to live out of doors; but the India-rubber is certainly a great improvement on tents that get soaked through."

"I like it," said Edith, "because it rubs things out. When I draw a house and it's all wrong, my piece of India-rubber will take it away, and then I can make another one on the paper."

"That is the very smallest of its uses," replied Miss Harson, smiling at the little girl's earnestness, "and yet we find it a great convenience. An English writer, speaking of it when it was first known in England, said that he had seen a substance that would efface from paper the marks of a black-lead pencil, and he thought it must be of use to those who practiced drawing."

"How funny that sounds!" exclaimed Malcolm. "Why, I couldn't get along without my India-rubber when I make mistakes,"

"You might," said his governess, "if you had some stale bread to rub with; for people have gotten along without a great many things which they now think necessary."

"Miss Harson," said Clara, "won't you tell us, please, how they get the caoutch--whatever it is--and make it into India-rubber?"

"I will," was the laughing reply, "when you can say the word properly. C-a-o-u-t-c-h-o-u-c--koochook."

As Clara said, Miss Harson made things so easy to understand! and in a very short time the hard word was mastered.

"As I have never seen the sap gathered," continued the young lady, "I shall have to read you an account of it, instead of telling you from my own experience; but the description is so plain that I think we shall all be able to understand it very well: 'At certain seasons of the year the natives visit some islands in the river Amazon that for many months are covered with water. As soon as the water subsides and a footing can be obtained the Indians arrive in parties, to seek for the trees. The Indian who comes every morning to collect the juice from the trunk has a number of trees allotted to him, and goes the round of the whole. The previous night he has made a long, deep cut in the bark of each and hung an earthen vessel beneath, to receive the thick, creamlike substance that trickles down. The vessel is filled by morning, and he pours the contents into one much larger and carries it to his hut. He is provided with a number of moulds of different shapes and sizes, and he dips them into the juice and puts them aside to dry. They are then dipped again, and the process is continued until the coat of India-rubber on the mould is of sufficient thickness. It is made black by passing it through the smoke of burning palm-nuts. The moulds are broken and taken out, leaving the India-rubber ready for sale, and pretty much as we used to see it in the shops before the people of this country had learned how to work it.'"

"That seems easy enough," said Malcolm, "but how do they make it into gutta-percha?"

"Gutta-percha is not made," replied his governess, "and it is taken from an entirely different tree, the Icosandra gutta, which grows in Southern Asia. The milky fluid is procured in the same way, but it is placed in vessels to evaporate, and the solid substance left at the bottom is the gutta-percha. It is not elastic, like India-rubber, and is called 'vegetable leather' because of its toughness and leathery appearance. It was discovered by an English traveler a long time before it was supposed to have any useful properties, but now it is considered a very valuable material. The wonderful submarine telegraph could not convey its messages between the Old World and the New were not its wires protected from injury by a coating of gutta-percha. Its unyielding nature and its not being elastic render it the very material needed. The long straps used in working machines are also made of gutta-percha, and this is another instance where its non-elasticity gives it the preference over India-rubber."

"And what is vulcanite?" asked Clara.

"It is caoutchouc mixed with sulphur. Unless a small quantity of brimstone is added in the manufacture of overshoes, they become soft when exposed to heat and hardened when exposed to cold; but it was discovered that the sulphur will keep them from being affected by changes in temperature. When a large amount of sulphur is used, the India-rubber, becomes as hard as horn or wood, and this is the substance called vulcanite. Now the gum is imported in masses, to be wrought over by our skillful mechanics."

The children were very much pleased to find that they had learned the nature of three important articles--India-rubber, gutta-percha and vulcanite-- and they thought it would be quite easy to remember the differences between them.

"And now," said Miss Harson, "the last of these useful trees--the cow tree, or milk tree--is the most curious one of all. Like the caoutchouc, it is a native of South America; but the sap is a rich fluid that answers for food, like milk. It is a fine-looking tree with oblong, pointed leaves about ten inches in length and a fleshy fruit containing one or two nuts. The sap is the most valuable part; and when incisions are made in the trunk of the tree, there is an abundant flow of thick milk-like sap, which is described as having an agreeable and balmy smell. The German traveler Humboldt drank it from the shell of a calabash, and the natives dip their bread of maize or cassava in it. This milk is said to be very fattening; and when exposed to the air, it thickens into a substance which the people call cheese."

"Milk and cheese from a tree!" exclaimed Malcolm. "Do you think we'd like them as well as ours, Miss Harson?"

"No," was the reply, "I do not think we should; but if we had never known any other kind, it would be quite a different matter, and the traveler says that both smell and taste are agreeable. The sap, it seems, is like curdled milk, and the natives say that they can tell, from the thickness and color of the foliage, the trunks that yield the most juice. This wonderful tree will be found growing on the side of a barren rock, and its large, woody roots can scarcely penetrate into the stone. For several months of the year not a single shower moistens its foliage. Its branches then appear dead and dried; but when the trunk is pierced, there flows from it a sweet and nourishing milk. It is at the rising of the sun that this vegetable fountain is most abundant. The negroes and natives are then seen hastening from all quarters, furnished with large bowls to receive the milk, which grows yellow and thickens at its surface. Some empty their bowls while under the tree itself; others carry the juice home to their children."

"Isn't it funny," said Edith, laughing, "to go and get their breakfasts from a tree? I wish we had some milk trees here."

"But you would not find it pleasant," replied their governess, "to have some other things that are always found where the milk tree grows. The intense heat and the swarms of mosquitoes and biting flies, the serpents and jaguars and other disagreeable and dangerous creatures, make life in that region anything but pleasant, and the curious vegetation and delicious fruits are not worth the suffering inflicted by all these torments."

On hearing of these drawbacks the children soon decided that their own dear home was the best, and no longer envied the possessors even of the cow tree.

CHAPTER XIV.

HOME AND ABROAD: LINDEN, CAMPHOR, BEECH.

"Now," said Miss Harson to her expectant flock, "it is to be hoped that our foreign wanderings among such wonderful trees have not spoiled you for home trees, as there are still a number of them which we have not yet examined."

"No indeed!" they assured her; "they liked to hear about them all, and they were going to try and remember everything she told them about the trees."

Their governess said that would be too much to expect, and if they remembered the most important things she would be quite satisfied,

"We will take the linden, lime, or basswood, tree--for it has all three of these names--this evening," she continued, "and there are nine or ten species of the tree, which are found in America, Europe and Western Asia. It is a very handsome, regular-looking tree with rich, thick masses of foliage that make a deep shade. The leaves are heart-shaped and very finely veined, have sharply-serrated edges and are four or five inches long. The leaf-stalk is half the length of the leaf. It blooms in July and August, and the flowers are yellowish white and very fragrant; when an avenue of limes is in blossom, the whole atmosphere is filled with a delightful perfume which can hardly be described."

"There are no lime trees here, are there?" asked Clara.

"No," was the reply, "I do not think there are any in this neighborhood; but they grow abundantly not many miles away. Our native trees are not so pretty as the English lime, which, clothed with softer foliage, has a smaller leaf and a neater and more elegant spray. Ours bears larger and more conspicuous flowers, in heavier clusters, but of inferior sweetness. Both species are remarkable for their size and longevity. The young leaves of the lime are of a bright fresh tint that contrasts strongly with the very dark color of the branches; and these branches are so finely divided that their beauty is seen to the greatest advantage when winter has stripped them bare of leaves.

"'The linden has in all ages been celebrated for the fragrance of its flowers and the excellence of the honey made from them. The famous Mount Hybla was covered with lime trees. The aroma from its flowers is like that of mignonette; it perfumes the whole atmosphere, and is perceptible to the inhabitants of all the beehives within a circuit of a mile. The real linden honey is of a greenish color and delicious taste when taken from the hive immediately after the trees have been in blossom, and is often sold for more than the ordinary kind. There is a forest in Lithuania that abounds in lime trees, and here swarms of wild bees live in the hollow trunks and collect their honey from the lime.'"

[Illustration: LEAF AND FLOWER OF LIME TREE (Tilia).]

"What fun it would be, if we were there, to go and get it!" exclaimed Malcolm. "But don't bees make honey from the lime trees that grow in this country, too, Miss Harson?"

"Certainly they do; and the beekeepers look anxiously forward to the blossoming of the trees, because they provide such abundant supplies for the busy swarms. The flowers have other uses, too, besides the making of honey: the Swiss are said to obtain a favorite beverage from them, and in the South of France an infusion of the blossoms is taken for colds and hoarseness, and also for fever. 'Active boys climb to the topmost branches and gather the fragrant flowers, which their mothers catch in their aprons for that purpose. An avenue of limes has been ravaged and torn in pieces by the eagerness of the people to gather the blossoms, and they are often made into tea which is a soft sugary beverage in taste a little like licorice.'"

"How queer," said Clara, "to make tea from flowers!"

"Is it any queerer," asked her governess, "than to make it from leaves? I should think that the flowers might even be better, and yet I should scarcely like lime-tea that tastes like licorice."

The children, though, seemed to think that they would like it, and Miss Harson had very little doubt that such would be the case.

"Both the bark and the wood of the lime tree are valuable," she continued. "The fibres of the bark are strong and firm, and make excellent ropes and cordage. In Sweden and Russia they are made into a kind of matting that is very useful for packing-purposes and in protecting delicate plants from the frost. 'The manufacture of this useful material is carried on in the summer, close by the woods and forests where the lime trees grow in abundance. As soon as the sap begins to ascend freely the bark parts from the wood and can be taken away with ease. Great strips are then peeled off and steeped in water until they separate into layers; the layers are still further divided into smaller strips or ribbons, and are hung up in the shade of the wood, generally on the very tree itself from which they have been taken. After a time they are woven into the matting and sent to market for sale. The Swedish fishermen also manufacture it into a coarse thread for fishing-nets, and from the fibres of the young shoots the Russian peasant makes the strong shoes he wears, using the outer bark for the soles. In Italy the garments of the poorer people are often made of cloth woven from this material."

"Why, people can fairly live on trees," said Malcolm. "I didn't know that they were good for anything but shade--except the trees that have fruit and nuts on 'em."

"There is a great deal for us all to learn of the works of the Creator," replied Miss Harson, "and the blessing of trees is not half known. The wood of the lime is said never to be worm-eaten; it is very soft and smooth and of a pale-yellow color. It is used for the famous Tunbridge ware, and is called the carver's tree, because, as the poet says,

"'Smooth linden best obeys The carver's chisel--best his curious work Displays in nicest touches.'

"The fruits and flowers carved for the choir of St. Paul's cathedral in London are done in lime-wood.

"So numerous are the purposes to which the bark, wood, leaves and blossoms of the lime, or linden, tree can be applied that centuries ago it was called the tree of a thousand uses. Linden is the name by which it is always known on the continent of Europe, and there it is indeed a magnificent tree, forming the most delightful avenues and branching colonnades. One of the principal streets in Berlin is called 'Unter den Linden.' In the Middle Ages, when the Swiss and the Flemings were always struggling for liberty, it was their custom to plant a lime tree on the field of battle, and many of these old trees still remain and have been the subject of ballads and poetical effusions:

"'The stately lime, smooth, gentle, straight and fair.'"

"Is there any story about it, Miss Harson?"

"No," was the reply, "not much of a story; only descriptions of some very large and very ancient trees. One of these, the old linden tree of Soleure, in Switzerland, was spoken of by an English traveler two hundred years ago as 'right noble and wondrous to behold. A bower composed of its branches is capable of holding three hundred persons sitting at ease; it has also a fountain set about with many tables formed solely of the boughs, to which men ascend by steps; and all is kept so accurately and thick that the sun never looks into it.'"

"It is just like a tent," said Malcolm, "it must be pleasant to sit by the fountain. Wouldn't you like it, Miss Harson?"

"I am sure I should," replied his governess; "and I should also like to see the famous lime tree of Zurich, the boughs of which will shelter five hundred persons. At Augsburg, in Germany, feasts and weddings have often been celebrated under the shade of some venerable limes that branch out to an immense distance. In early times divine honors were paid to them as emblems of immortality. And now," said Miss Harson, "the last of these famous trees is a noble lime tree which grew on the farm belonging to the ancestors of Linnaeus, the great naturalist, beneath the shade of which he played in childhood, and from which his ancestors derived their surname. That noble tree still blossoms from year to year, beautiful in every change of seasons."

"Lime, linden and basswood," said Clara--"three names to remember for one tree. But didn't you say, Miss Harson, that it's always called basswood in our country?"

"Often, but not always. The name linden is quite common with us, and it will be well for you to remember that it is also called lime, so that when you go to Europe you will know what is meant by lime and linden."

The children laughed at this idea, for it seemed very funny to think of a little girl like Clara going to Europe, but, as their governess told them, little girls did go constantly; besides, this was the time to learn what would be of use to them when they were grown.

"The fragrant lime," said Miss Harson, "has a relative in Asia whose acquaintance I wish you to make, and you know it already in one of its products, which is common in every household. It is also very fragrant--or rather, I should say, it has a strong aromatic odor which is very reviving in cases of faintness or illness, although it has quite a contrary effect on insects, particularly on mosquitoes. I should like to have some one tell me what this white, powerful substance is."

This was quite a conundrum, and for a little while the children were extremely puzzled over its solution; but presently Clara asked,

"Do the moths hate it too, Miss Harson? And isn't it camphor?"

"Camphor doesn't grow on a tree," said Malcolm, in a superior tone; "it is dug out of the earth."

"I have never read of any camphor-mines," replied his governess, laughing, "and I think you will find that camphor--which is just what I meant--is obtained from the trunk of a tree."

"Like India-rubber?" asked Edith.

"No, dear, not like India-rubber, for it grows in even a more curious way than that, masses of it being found in the trunk of the camphor tree--not in the form of sap, but in lumps, as we use it."

"I thought it was like water," said Edith, in a puzzled tone.

"So it is when dissolved in alcohol, as we generally have it; but it is also used in lumps to drive away moths and for various other purposes. But I will tell you all about the tree, which grows in the islands of Sumatra and Borneo and bears the botanical name Dryobalanops camphora. The camphor is also called barus camphor, to distinguish it from the laurus, of which I will tell you afterward, and it is of a better quality and more easily obtained. The tree grows in the forests of these East Indian islands and is remarkable for its majestic size, dense foliage and magnolia-like flowers. The trunk rises as high as ninety feet without a single branch, and within it are cavities, sometimes a foot and a half long, which cannot be perceived until the bark is split open. These cavities contain the camphor in clear crystalline masses, and with it an oil known as camphor oil, that is thought by some to be camphor in an immature form. But the oil, even when crystallized by artificial means, does not produce such good camphor as that already solidified in the tree."

"To think," exclaimed Clara, "of camphor growing in that way! But how do they get it out, Miss Harson? Do they cut great holes in the trunk of the tree?"

"No, dear; I have just read to you that the camphor cannot be seen until the bark is split open, and the grand trees have to be cut down. But to do this is no easy matter. The hard, close-grained timber requires days of hewing and sawing to get it severed. The masses of roots are as unyielding as iron, and run twisting through the soil to the distance of sixty yards. Even at their farthest extremity they are as thick as a man's thigh."

"I shouldn't think the camphor was worth all that trouble," said Malcolm; "it don't seem to amount to much, any wary."

"It is more valuable than you suppose," replied Miss Harson; "for, besides preserving furs and woolen fabrics from the devouring moth, it protects the contents of cabinets and museums from the attacks of the minute creatures that prey upon the dried specimens of the naturalist. Not any of the insect tribe can endure the powerful scent of the camphor, and they either retreat before it or are killed by it. But its principal value is in medicine. It is used both internally and externally. It acts as a nervous stimulant, and is a favorite domestic remedy.--So you see, Malcolm, that camphor really amounts to a great deal, and we could not very well do without it."

"How can people tell when there is any camphor inside the tree?" asked Clara.

"They cannot tell," was the reply, "until the trunk is split open, although a tribe of men in Sumatra say that they know before-hand, by a kind of magic, which is the right tree to cut down. But the beautiful, stately tree is often wasted in vain, and after all their hard work the camphor-seekers find the cavities of the split-up trunk filled with a thick black substance like pitch instead of the pure white camphor."

"Poor things!" said Edith, pityingly; "that's too bad."

"Camphor is found in many trees and shrubs," continued her governess, "but in all others except the camphor tree of Sumatra and Borneo it has to be distilled from the wood and roots. The camphor-laurel, which is about the size of an English oak, is the most important of these trees. It grows abundantly in the Chinese island of Formosa, and 'camphor mandarin' is the title of a rich Chinaman who pays the government for the privilege of extracting all the camphor, which he sends to other countries at a large profit. Every part of this tree is full of camphor, and the tree gives out, when bruised, a strong perfume.

"The European bay tree, which is more like an immense shrub, is also a member of this singular tribe, and its leaves have the strong family flavor. They were used in medicine, as well as the berries, before the camphor-laurel became known in Europe; in the time of Queen Elizabeth the floors of the better sort of houses were strewed with bay-leaves instead of being carpeted as now. The bay was an emblem of victory in old Roman times, and victorious generals were crowned with it. A wreath of this laurel, with the berries on, was placed on the head of a favorite poet in the Middle Ages, and in this way came the title 'poet-laureate'--laureatus,' crowned with laurel.'

"Do you remember," continued Miss Harson, "the tall, straight tree that I showed you yesterday when we were out in the woods--the one with a fluted trunk? What was its name?"

"I know!" said Malcolm, quite excited. "Think of the seashore! Beach! That's what I told myself to remember."

"A very good idea," replied his governess, laughing; "only you must not spell it with an a, like the seashore, for it is b-e-e-c-h.--The fluted, or ribbed, shaft of this grand-looking tree is often sixty or seventy feet high, and, although it is found in its greatest perfection in England, it is a common tree in most of the woods in this country. For depth of shade no tree is equal to the beech, and its long beautiful leaves, with their close ridges and serrated edges, are very much like those of the chestnut. The leaves are of a light, fresh green and very neat and perfect, because they are so seldom attacked by insects; they remain longer on the branches than those of any deciduous tree, and give a cheerful air to the wood in winter. In the autumn they change to a light yellow-brown, which makes a pretty contrast to the reds and greens and purples of other trees. The branches start out almost straight from the tree, but they very soon curve and turn regularly upward. Every small twig turns in the same direction, making the long leaf-buds at the end look like so many little spears. I showed you these 'stuck-up' buds when we were looking at the tree, and you noticed how different they were from the other trees."

Yes, the children remembered it; and it always seemed to them particularly nice to have part of the talk out of doors and the rest in the house.

"Doesn't the beech tree have nuts?" asked Malcolm. "John says it does."

"Yes," replied Miss Harson; "it has tiny three-cornered nuts which seem particularly small for so large a tree. But these nuts are eagerly devoured by pigeons, partridges and squirrels. Bears are said to be very fond of them, and swine fatten very rapidly upon them. Most varieties are so small as not to repay the trouble of gathering, drying and opening them. Fortunately, this is not the case with all, as it is a delicious nut. In France the beech-nut is much used for making oil, which is highly valued for burning in lamps and for cooking. In parts of the same country the nuts, roasted, serve as a substitute for coffee."

"I'd like to find some when they're ripe," said Clara, "if they are little."

"We will have a search for them, then," was the reply, "when the time comes.--The flowers which produce these little nuts are very showy and grow in roundish tassels, or heads, which hang by thread-like, silky stalks, one or two inches long, from the midst of the young leaves of a newly-opened bud. A traveler says of these leaves, 'We used always to think that the most luxurious and refreshing bed was that which prevails universally in Italy, and which consists entirely of a pile of mattresses filled with the luxuriant spathe of the Indian corn; which beds have the advantage of being soft as well as elastic, and we have always found the sleep enjoyed on them to be particularly sound and restorative. But the beds made of beech-leaves are really no whit behind them in these qualities, whilst the fragrant smell of green tea, which the leaves retain, is most gratifying. The objection to them is the slight crackling noise which the leaves occasion as the individual turns in bed, but this is no inconvenience at all; or if so in any degree, it is an inconvenience which is overbalanced by the advantages of this most luxurious couch."

"But how funny," said Malcolm, "to sleep on leaves! That's what the Babes in the Wood did."

"No," replied Clara, very earnestly, "they didn't sleep on leaves, you know; but when they had laid down and gone to sleep, the robins came and covered them with leaves."

"Yes," chimed in little Edith; "I like that way best, because they'd be so cold in the woods."

"And that really was the case," said Miss Harson, after listening with a smile to this discussion, "although there were probably leaves on the ground for the children to lie upon. A bed of leaves is not a bad thing where there are no mattresses, and such a bed is often used as a matter of course. You will remember my reading to you about the beds which the Finland mothers make for their children of the leaves of the canoe-birch. 'Leafy beds' are no strange thing--not mere poetry."

CHAPTER XV.

THE TENT AND THE LOCUSTS.

There came a bright balmy day in May when the children found a delightful surprise awaiting them. The tent in the woods, which had been proposed on the day when birch-twigs were found to be eatable, was almost forgotten--or if thought of, it was as a thing that could not possibly be--when, on the day in question, Miss Harson took her charges out as usual, and led them to a very pretty cleared space with a fringe of rocks and trees all around it. But on this spot, which hitherto had been quite bare, there now stood some sort of a little house different from other houses and quite pretty.

"It's a tent!" exclaimed Malcolm. "Who put it there, I should like to know, on our land?"

"Are there gypsies here, Miss Harson?" whispered Clara, rather fearfully.

But the young lady walked deliberately up to the entrance of the tent and invited her little flock to come inside.

"I know the gentleman who had it put here," she said, "and he is quite willing that we should use it; but he will not give any one else this liberty."

"I think I know him too," said Malcolm as he walked in after Miss Harson.

"And I!"--"And I!" exclaimed the little girls. "It is our own papa. How very kind of him!"

"Yes," replied their governess; "he said, when I spoke of a tent, that it would be a good thing for the wood-ramblers to have a place of shelter when they were over-taken by a sudden shower, and also a place in which to rest comfortably when they were tired; and this pretty tent, you see, is all ready for us at any time."

It was a very nice tent indeed, having a long cushioned seat inside, two little rocking-chairs that were at once appropriated, a small table, and a bracket with books on it. On the table there was a round basket of oranges, which made every one thirsty at once.

"I do believe," said Malcolm, suddenly, "that it's made of India-rubber."

"Not the orange, I hope?" replied Miss Harson, while the little sisters looked up in surprise.

An India-rubber orange was a thing to be laughed at, though not to be eaten, and the children were in such a state of glee over this pleasant surprise that they were ready to laugh almost at nothing.

Presently their governess said,

"Malcolm means the tent, of course; and he is quite right, for the covering is India-rubber cloth."

"But why isn't it dark and ugly, like the waterproofs?" was the next question.

"Simply because it need not be so, and it is prettier to have it white or of this pale gray. But these shades are too conspicuous for overshoes or waterproof cloaks, so the latter are made as dark as possible. The caoutchoue, you know, is naturally white or very light colored."

"How do they make the cloth?" asked Malcolm.

"It is first made as cloth," was the reply; "then a thin coating of India-rubber is spread over two layers of it. The cloth is then put together and pressed between rollers, so that the two pieces firmly adhere, with the caoutchoue between them. No rain can penetrate such a screen as this,"

It was delightful to know that they would be safe and dry in case of a shower, and the children thought it must be just the prettiest tent that ever was made. The cushioned seat was covered with scarlet, and so were the little chairs, which Clara and Edith knew were meant for them; the edges of the cloth were scalloped with the same bright color, and there was even a rug to match spread in front of the "divan," as Miss Harson laughingly said the cushioned seat must be called.

"Haven't we 'most come to the end of the trees?" asked Clara. "I never thought that there were so many different kinds,"

"Look around and see if you feel acquainted with them all," replied her governess.

They had left the tent after quite a long "sitting," and were now on their way to the house.

Clara's first glance, on doing as she had been directed, fell on three trees by the side of a fence, that were different from any they had yet studied.

"What do you notice about them?" continued Miss Harson; "for I wish you to use your own eyes and thoughts as much as possible."

"Why, the trunk is dark gray, and it isn't smooth, but it looks as if some one had dug out long, thin pieces of bark."

"We will call it 'deeply furrowed,'" said her governess, "as that is a better expression; but your description is very good indeed."

"The leaves are ever so pretty," said Malcolm--"so many of 'em on one stem!--and the green looks as if it was just made."

"You mean by that, I suppose," replied Miss Harson, "that it is a very fresh tint; and we are seeing it in its first beauty now. This is the locust tree, and May is its time for leafing out in the tenderest of greens. The pinnate--from pinna, Latin for feather'--leaves are composed of from nine to twenty-five leaflets, which are egg-shaped, with a short point, very smooth, light green above and still lighter beneath. These leaves are much liked by cattle, and they are said to be very nutritious to them."

"How can you remember everything so, Miss Harson?" asked Malcolm, lost in wonder, as the young lady, looking up at the trees, said these things as if they had been written there. John had declared that she talked like a book, and this seemed more like it than ever.

"Oh no," was the laughing reply; "I do not remember everything, Malcolm, and perhaps it is just as well that I do not. But I will not tax my memory any more about the locust just now; we can take it up again this evening."

"I should like to know," exclaimed Clara, after some thought, "why a tree is called locust, when a locust is such a disagreeable insect?"

"I am afraid that I cannot tell you," replied Miss Harson, "unless the color of the leaves is similar to that of the 'disagreeable insect,' which is really very handsome, or unless the insects are very partial to the tree; I have seen no explanation of it. But the tree itself is very much admired, with its profusion of pinnate leaves and racemes of flowers that fill the air with the most agreeable odors."

"What color are the flowers, Miss Harson?" asked Malcolm.

"This description will tell you," was the reply. "The tree is not pretty in winter, and has no promise of beauty until 'May hangs on these withered boughs a green drapery that hides all their deformity; she infuses into their foliage a perfection of verdure that no other tree can rival, and a beauty in the forms of its leaves that renders it one of the chief ornaments of the groves and waysides. June weaves into this green foliage pendent clusters of flowers of mingled brown and white, filling the air with fragrance and enticing the bee with odors as sweet as from groves of citron and myrtle.'"

"That sounds pretty," said Clara, who liked imposing sentences, "but brown and white are not very handsome colors for flowers."

"The white is certainly prettier without the mixture of brown," replied her governess, "but we have to take our flowers ready-made, and can hardly expect them to be beautiful and fragrant too. The separate blossoms are shaped like those of the pea and bean; they hang in long clusters somewhat resembling bunches of grapes. The leaves--or, rather, leaflets--are very sensitive and have a habit of folding over one another in wet and dull weather, and also in the night--a habit that is peculiar to all the members of the acacia family, to which the locust belongs."

"I should think it ought to belong to the pea family," said Malcolm, "if the flowers are shaped like pea-blossoms."

"So it does," replied Miss Harson--"or, rather, to the bean family, of which the pea is a member, on account of its blossoms; but the acacia, like many others, is a brother, or sister, on account of its leaves as well as its blossoms. The peculiar distinction of this family is that its flowers are butterfly-shaped or its fruit in pods, and it often possesses both these characters. By one or the other all the plants of the family are known, and the butterfly-shaped flowers are of a character not to be mistaken, as they are found in no other family. It includes herbs, shrubs and trees--an immense and perfectly natural family, distributed throughout almost every part of the globe. There are at present in all not less than thirty-seven hundred species. So you see that the locust tree is certainly rich in relations."

The children thought that it must have some family claim on almost every plant in the world.

"Do you remember that in the story of the Prodigal Son, told by our Lord, it is said that the bad son became so poor that he wanted to eat the 'husks' that the swine ate? Those 'husks' were the fruit of a Syrian member of this family.

The tree is the carob tree, of which you have here a picture--a fine large tree bearing a sweet pod containing the seeds. I have seen these pods for sale in this country, and foolishly called St. John's bread, as if the 'locusts' eaten by John the Baptist were pods of a locust tree, and not insect locusts."

"Yes," said Malcolm, "I have tasted those pods, and they are real sweet; but I wouldn't care to make a breakfast from them."

"I like calling the flowers 'butterfly-shaped,'" said Clara, "because that is just what the pea and bean-blossoms look like; though Kitty calls 'em 'little ladies in hoods.' Isn't that funny, Miss Harson?"

"It is very quaint, I think, but I do not dislike it: it is like seeing faces in pansies; and some people are full of these odd imaginations. There is a kind of locust, called the clammy-barked, found in the Southern parts of the United States, which is a smaller tree than the common locust and has large pale-pink flowers, while the rose acacia is a very beautiful flowering shrub. The sweet, or honey, locust is another variety, which is also called the three-thorned acacia, because the thorns consist of one long spine with two shorter ones projecting out of it, like little branches, near its base. This is said to display much of the elegance of the tropical acacia in the minute division and symmetry of its compound leaves. These are of a light and brilliant green and lie flat upon the branches, giving them a fan-like appearance such as we observe in the hemlock."

"But why is it called honey-locust?" asked Malcolm. "Do the bees make honey in the trunk?"

"No," replied his governess; "the name comes from the sweetness of the pulp around the seeds, which ripen in large flat pods, and of which boys and girls are fond. But the flowers of this species are only small greenish aments. Locust-wood is very durable, and, as it will bear exposure to all kinds of weather, it is much used in shipbuilding and as posts for gates. It is thought that the shittah and shittim wood of the Bible, of which Moses made the greater part of the tables, altars and planks of the tabernacle, was the same as the black acacia found in the deserts of Arabia and about Mount Sinai and the mountains which border on the Red Sea, and is so hard and solid as to be almost incorruptible.

"And now," added Miss Harson, "reading of the numerous relations of the locust, considering that 'the acacia, not less valued for its airy foliage and elegant blossoms than for its hard and durable wood; the braziletto, logwood and rosewoods of commerce; the laburnum; the furze and the broom, both the pride of the otherwise dreary heaths of Europe; the bean, the pea, the vetch, the clover, the trefoil, the lucerne--all staple articles of culture by the farmer--are so many species of Leguminosae, and that the gums Arabic and Senegal, kino and various precious medicinal drugs, not to mention indigo, the most useful of all dyes, are products of other species,--it will be perceived that it would be difficult to point out an order with greater claims upon the attention.'"

CHAPTER XVI.

THE WALNUT FAMILY AND THE AILANTHUS.

"The walnut family," said Miss Harson, "with the ugly name Juglandaceae, are distinguished by pinnate, or compound, leaves, which have an aromatic odor when crushed, and by blossoms in catkins. Of these trees, the black walnut is one of the handsomest and most highly prized."

"Are there any of them here?" asked Malcolm.

"No," was the reply; "I do not think you have ever seen one. They are more common in the western part of the Middle States and in the Western States; in Ohio particularly they grow to a very large size. Solitary trees are sometimes seen in this part of the country, and the branches, extending themselves horizontally to a great distance, spread out into a spacious head, which gives them a very majestic appearance. The trunk is rough and furrowed, and the leaves have from six to ten pairs of leaflets and an odd one. They are smooth, strongly serrated and rather pointed; the color is a light, bright green. The catkins are green, from four to seven inches long, and hang from the axils of the last year's leaves. The leaves are much longer than those of the locust, and the leaf-stalk is downy. The nut, which is very oily, is shaped like an English walnut, but resembles it in no other way, as the shell is very thick and dark-colored. When thoroughly dried, the black walnut is very much liked--as I think some witnesses here could testify--and is used in making candy."

"And just the nicest kind of candy, too," said the children, with one voice.

Their governess smiled, for this was very much her own opinion.

"You do not know," she continued, "how strangely these nuts grow. They have an outer husk, or rind, which when green is hard and has a very pleasant smell; the tree then seems to be covered with green balls. As the nuts ripen this outer part becomes so dark that it is almost black and grows soft and spongy. A rich brown dye is made from it. Black-walnut wood has long been famous for its beauty, and it grows deeper and darker with age. It is handsomely shaded and takes a fine polish, and this, with its durability, makes it very valuable for furniture. Posts made of it will last a long time, and it can be put to almost any use for which hard-wood is available.

"The walnut tree has a great variety of good qualities in addition to its fine appearance and generous shade. From the kernel a valuable oil may be obtained for use in cookery and in lamps. Bread has also been made from the kernels. The spongy husk of the nuts is used as dyestuff. It thus unites almost all the qualities desirable in a tree--beauty, gracefulness and richness of foliage in every period of its growth; bark and husks which may be employed in an important art; fruit valuable as food; wood unsurpassed in durability and in elegance."

"I like English walnuts," said Clara, "they have such thin, pretty shells; and papa, you know, can open them in just two halves with a knife."

"Once," said Miss Harson, "I had a little bag sent to me made of two very large walnut shells with blue silk between, and in this bag there was a pair of kid gloves rolled up very tight."

"Oh!" exclaimed the children. It sounded like a fairy-tale, but they knew that it was true, because Miss Harson said that it had really happened. They were very much surprised, though, that a bag could be made of nutshells, and that a pair of gloves could be crowded into so small a compass.

"Did it come from England?" asked Malcolm.

"No," replied his governess; "it was sent to me from the island of Madeira, where these nuts grow so abundantly that they have often been called Madeira-nuts. It also grows abundantly in Europe, and the nuts are used for dessert, pickling, and many other purposes, while the poorer classes often depend largely on them for food."

"Do they eat 'em instead of bread?" asked Edith. "I'd like that; they're ever so much nicer!"

"Perhaps you would not think so if you had hardly anything else to eat; you would get tired of them then. In many places on the continent of Europe the roads are lined with walnut trees for miles together, and in the proper season the people may feast upon the fruit as much as they like. A person, it is said, once traveled from Florence to Geneva and ate nothing by the way but walnuts; but I must say that I should not like to do it. One species bears a nut as large as an egg; but if kept any time, it will shrink to half its natural size. The shell of this great walnut, we are told, is sometimes used for making little ornamental boxes to hold gloves and small fancy-articles; so you see that mine was not the only glove-bag made of two walnut-shells."

"How pretty they must be!" said Clara. "I should like to see one."

"I think that I can make one when I get a large nut, and I shall be glad to show you how it is done."

This was a delightful prospect, and the children volunteered to save for that especial purpose all the large nuts they could find.

"The English walnut tree," continued Miss Harson, "is a native of Persia or the North of China, and the long pinnated leaves seem to mark its Oriental origin; but it has taken very kindly to its European home. In some parts of Germany the walnut trees were considered to be such a valuable possession that no young man was allowed to marry until he owned a certain number; and if one tree was cut down, another was always planted."

"Don't they grow in this country?" asked Malcolm.

"Not very often in our more northern States," was the reply, "for the climate here is too cold for them; but at a house where I visited there was an English walnut tree in the garden, and it seemed to do very well. The nuts were always gathered while they were green, and made into pickles."

This was considered quite dreadful, for ripe nuts were certainly a great deal better than pickles.

"But there was a great deal of uncertainty about having the ripe nuts, for there were bad boys all around who would not have hesitated to rob the tree. Besides, pickled walnuts are considered a great delicacy by those who eat such things. There are some other ways, too, of using the nuts, which you would not like any better. One of these is to make them into oil, as the people do in the South of Europe; this oil is used to burn in their lamps and as an article of food. 'In Piedmont, among the light-hearted peasantry, cracking the walnuts and taking them from the shell is a holiday proceeding. The peasants, with their wives and children, assemble in the evening, after their day's work is over, in the kitchen of some ch 鈚 eau where the walnuts have been gathered, and where their services are required. They sit round a table, and at each end is a man with a small mallet, who cracks the walnuts and passes them on; the rest of the party take them out of their shells. At supper-time the table is cleared, and a repast of dried fruit, vegetables and wine is set out. The remainder of the evening is spent in singing and dancing. The crushing and pressing of the nuts, for oil, take place when the whole harvest is in.'"

"But don't walnuts come from California? Our grocer said he had California nuts," remarked Malcolm.

"Yes; that wonderful country is beginning to supply us with English walnuts."

"Are you going to tell us a story, Miss Harson?" asked Edith, hopefully.

"I have no story, dear," was the reply, "but there is something here which you may like about birds stealing the nuts."

Of course they would like this; for if there was to be no story, birds and stealing promised to furnish a good substitute.

"'Birds are as fond of walnuts as we are,'" read Miss Harson, "'and rob the trees without any mercy. Not only the little titmouse, but the grave and solemn rook'--a kind of crow, you remember--'is not above paying a visit to the walnut tree and stealing all he can find. There is a walnut tree growing in a garden the owner of which may be said to have planted it for the benefit of the rooks. Not that he had any such purpose, but, as it happens, he cannot help himself. The rooks begin a series of robberies as soon as the fruit is ripe, and carry them on with an adroitness that would be amusing but for the result. As many as fifty rooks come, one after the other, and each will carry off a walnut. The old ones are the most at home in the process, and the most daring. The bird approaches the tree and floats for a second in the air, as if occupied in finding out which of the walnuts will be the easiest to obtain; then, with a bold stroke, he darts at the one selected, and rarely misses his aim.

"'The young rooks are much more timid and not so successful. They settle on the branch and knock down a great many walnuts in their clumsy attempts to secure one. Even when the walnut has been obtained, the young rook is not sure of his prize: one of his older and stronger brethren is very likely to attack him and knock the walnut out of his bill. Then, by a dextrous swoop, the robber catches it up before it reaches the ground, and carries it off in triumph. The feasting ground of the rooks is the next field, and here they come to eat their walnuts. They crack the shell with their beaks and devour the kernel with great relish. Then, when one walnut is finished, they fly back to the tree for another. There is no chance for the owner of the garden, who does not think it worth while even to shake his tree: he knows there will not be a single walnut left.'"

"I should think not, with those greedy creatures," exclaimed Malcolm. "Why doesn't the man shoot 'em?"

"He probably thinks it would be of little use, when there are such numbers of the birds; besides, he may prefer losing his walnuts to disturbing them, for rooks are treated with great consideration in England, and there is no such wholesale destruction of birds as is seen here."

The rooks were certainly very comical, and the children thought this little account of their antics over the walnut tree the next best thing to a story.

"Another fine shade-tree," continued Miss Harson, "and one very much like the black walnut, is the butternut, or oil-nut, tree. It is low and broad-headed, spreading into several large branches; the leaves are pinnate, like those of the walnut, but have not so many leaflets. The nut has an entirely different taste, and is even more oily. To many persons it is not at all agreeable. It is a great favorite, though, with country-boys, and in October, when the kernel is ripe, they may be seen with deeply-stained hands and faces, as the thin, leathery husks when handled leave plentiful traces. The butternut is not round like the walnut, but oblong, and pointed at the end; it is about two inches in length and marked by deep furrows and sharp irregular ridges. It is very pretty when sawn across in slices, and looks like scroll-saw work.--We shall have to get some, Malcolm, for you to practice on with your saw."

As his scroll-saw was just then the delight of Malcolm's heart, he felt particularly interested in butternuts, and immediately mapped out in his mind something very beautiful to be wrought with them for his governess.

"The bark and the nutshells have long been used to give a brown color to wool, and the Shakers dye a rich purple with it. The bark of the trunk will give a black and that of the root a fawn-colored dye, while an inferior sugar has been made from the sap. The young half-grown nuts are much used for pickles. Butternut-wood is exceedingly handsome, of a pale, reddish tint, and durable when exposed to heat and moisture. It makes beautiful fronts for drawers and excellent light, tough and durable wooden bowls. It is also used for the panels of carriages, as well as for posts and rails. It is a more common tree than the walnut in our part of the country; there is a large one in front of a house a few miles from here which I will show you on our next drive."

"I am glad of it," said Clara, "for I can remember about the trees so much better when I have seen them. I wish we could see every one of the trees you have told us of, Miss Harson."

"Perhaps you will some day," replied her governess, "and you will then find that a little knowledge of them before-hand is a great help."

"Are there any more of the walnut family?" asked Malcolm.

"Yes, the hickory belongs to it; and this is a tree which is peculiar to America. The European walnut is more like it than any other. It is always a stately and elegant tree and very valuable for its timber. There are several varieties, which are much alike, the principal difference being in the nuts. You have all seen most of the trees and gathered the nuts. They are:

"1. The shellbark, with five large leaflets, a large nut, of which the husk is deeply grooved at the seams, and a rough, scaly trunk.

"2. The mocker-nut, with seven or nine leaflets, a hard, thick-shelled nut, and leaflets and twigs very downy when young, and strongly odorous.

"3. The pignut, with three, five or seven narrow leaflets, small, thin-shelled fruit and a pretty hard nut.

"4. The bitternut, with seven, nine or eleven small, narrow, serrated leaves, small fruit with long, prominent seams, bitter and thin-shelled nuts and very yellow buds.

"The shellbark is often called 'shagbark,' and it is the finest of the hickories and one that is seldom mistaken for any of the others. It may readily be distinguished by the shaggy bark of its trunk, the excellence of its globular fruit, its leaves, which are large and have five leaflets, and by its ovate, half-covered buds. It is a tall, slender tree with irregular branches, and the foliage seems to lie in masses of dense, dark green. But in October, when the nuts ripen, the leaves turn to orange-brown, and finally to the color of a russet apple; so that they do not add greatly to the beauty of the forest."

"But the nuts are good," said Malcolm. "Didn't we have fine times picking 'em up?"

"We did indeed," replied Miss Harson, "and I hope we shall again."

"How long will it be before they are ripe?" asked the little girls.

"Just about five months, I think."

"Oh dear!" was the reply; "that's so long to wait!"

"But you needn't wait," said their governess; "you can enjoy each season as it comes, and all the good things that our heavenly Father sends with it. Remember that, as you cannot expect ripe nuts in May or June, neither can you look for strawberries and roses in October. Tents are of very little use then, too."

"Oh!" exclaimed the children, to whom the tent was still a delightful novelty; and they decided not to wish just yet for nutting-time to come.

"The nut, as you have so often seen, is covered with a brown husk that is very thick and marked with four furrows, by which it separates into as many distinct pieces, one being larger than the rest. The nuts differ very much in size and shape, and also in hardness, but the best kinds have thin shells and soft kernels; they are also rounder and fuller than the poorer sorts. There is a peculiar sweetness in the taste of this nut when in its best condition, and it is quite equal to the European walnut. The wood of this tree is particularly valuable for fuel, and in old times, when wood-fires were the only kind known, a good hickory back-log was sure to be found on every hearth. It is the heaviest of our native woods, and the wise men say that it yields, pound for pound or cord for cord, more heat than any other, in any shape in which it may be consumed."

"But what a pity," said Clara, "to burn up trees that bear nuts! Why can't they take those that don't?"

"They are not so desirable for fuel," was the reply; "and when people own trees which they are willing to turn into money, they generally consider in what way they can get the most for them. Nuts which grow in the woods and fields are a very uncertain crop, of which every one seems to gather more than the owner, and it is therefore more profitable for him to cut his trees down and sell them for their wood, which the people in the cities and towns are so glad to get."

"What's the use," asked Malcolm, "of calling a tree such a name as mocker-nut? What does it mean?"

"That is just what I have not been able to find out," replied Miss Harson, "but it has an Indian sound, and it seems that the Indians used to make a black dye from the bark; so we will give them the credit for it. The name is not often used, for the tree is generally known as the white walnut. The nut is the largest of the hickories, being often from four to six inches around, and it is shaped somewhat like a pear. One variety, however, is known as the square nut. The shell is very thick and hard, but the kernel is sweet when once it is gotten out. This tree is as stately and finely-shaped as the shagbark. It varies from the other hickories in the number of its leaflets, which are seven or nine, the down on its leaves and recent shoots, the hardness of the husk and thickness of the nut, the roundness of its large covered buds, and the strong resinous odor in leaves, buds and husks. In its general appearance it resembles the shellbark, as well as in the fullness of its foliage and the size of its leaves. 'White-heart hickory' is a name often given to this species, because the wood is supposed, when young, to be whiter than that of any of the others,"

"Pignut is another beautiful name," said Malcolm, who was disposed to be critical. "Do pigs ever eat the nuts, Miss Harson?"

"I dare say that they do when they have the chance," was the reply, "as they delight in nuts; but that is said not to be the proper name for the species. Some of the nuts are shaped like a fresh fig, and 'fig-nut' seems to be the name originally intended. But there is a great variety in the shape of the nuts, as some are nearly round and others very irregular. They are alike, however, in having very hard, tough shells, and the kernel is not pleasant enough to repay the trouble of getting at it. These nuts are very apt to grow in pairs, and several bushels of them can be gathered from one tree."

"Aren't they good to eat?" asked Clara.

"Not at all good," replied her governess, "except to those who are not particular about what they eat; and this may be the reason for calling them 'pignuts,'"

"Bitternut doesn't sound much better," said Malcolm, again. "I wonder what that species has to say for itself?"

"Not very much, I am afraid, for it is sometimes called the bitter pignut, and even boys will not eat it, while squirrels refuse to feed on it when any other nut can be found. The shell of this nut is so thin that it can be broken in the fingers, but, as no one cares to break it, it is safer than many a thicker shell. It is intensely bitter, and well deserves its name. The tree, however, is handsome and the most graceful of all the hickories; the small, slender leaves give it the look of an ash, and the trunk is smoother than that of most large trees. In summer the finely-cut foliage is of a bright green, and in autumn it changes to a rich orange, which lasts after the other species have become russet and brown."

"Is there anything more about hickory trees?" said Clara.

"Only to speak of the great value of the wood," replied Miss Harson. "Its uses are almost endless. Great numbers of walking-sticks are made of it, as for this purpose no other native wood equals it in beauty and strength. It is next in value to white oak for making hoops; it makes the best screws, the smoothest and most durable handles for chisels, augurs, gimlets, axes, and many other common tools. As fuel, hickory is preferred to every other wood, burning freely, making a pleasant, brilliant fire and throwing out great heat. Charcoal made from it is heavier than that made from any other wood, but it is not considered more valuable than that of birch or alder. The ashes of hickories abound in alkali, and are considered better for the purpose of making soap than any other of the native woods, being next to those of the apple tree."

"There, Clara!" said Malcolm; "you see now why people cut down hickory trees. The nuts are nowhere, with all these other things."

"We have finished the walnut family," said Miss Harson, "but there is a tree that I wish to speak of here because of its long pinnate leaves, which appear to connect it with the walnuts and hickories. This is the ailanthus, a large tree which you have often seen in the village, and which used to be popular as a shade-tree. It is very clean-looking, for the only insect that will eat its leaves is the silkworm."

"Oh, Miss Harson!" exclaimed the children. "Are there real silkworms on 'em? and can we see 'em?"

"Why, do you not remember our talk about silkworms?" replied their governess. "I am sure I told you that they would not live here in the open air, but they do in China; and the ailanthus is a Chinese tree. It was planted in Great Britain over a hundred years ago for the express purpose of feeding silkworms, because a species of silkworm which was known to be hardy and capable of forming its cocoons in the English climate is attached to this tree and feeds upon its leaves. It was not successful, however, for silkworms, but as a stately and ornamental tree with tropical-looking foliage it was much admired. The ailanthus is quite common in this country as a wayside tree. It possesses a good deal of beauty, from the size and graceful sweep of its large compound leaves, that retain their brightness and verdure after midsummer, when our native trees have become dull. These leaves have nine or ten leaflets as large as a beech-leaf."

"Isn't that the tree that smells so in summer?" asked Clara, with a disgusted face.

"Yes; the greenish flowers have a particularly disagreeable odor, which is very strong and penetrating, and this is probably the reason why the tree has lost favor in so many places. But this is only during the season of blossoming, and for several months it is a beautiful Oriental-looking tree with every leaf perfect, while nearly all other foliage is more or less ravaged by insects."

CHAPTER XVII.

SOME BEAUTIFUL TREES: THE CHESTNUT AND HORSE-CHESTNUT.

The nearest trees to the tent, and standing just back of it, were two magnificent chestnuts, now in full leaf-beauty; and Miss Harson and her little flock stood admiring their majestic size and beautiful color.

"These are the handsomest trees yet," said Malcolm.

"I almost think so myself," replied his governess, gazing up into the rich green depths, "and I wish you particularly to notice these radiated--or star-like--tufts of foliage. The leaves, you see, are long, lengthened to a tapering point, serrated--or notched like a saw--at the edge, and of a bright and nearly pure green. Though arranged alternately, like those of the beech, on the recent branches, they are clustered in stars containing from five to seven leaves on the fruitful branches that grow out from the perfected wood. Now stand off a little and see how the foliage seems to be all in tufts, each composed of several long, pointed leaves drooping from the centre. The aments, too, with their light silvery-green tint, glisten beautifully on the darker leaves."

"How high do you think these trees are, Miss Harson?" asked Clara. "It makes me dizzy to look up to the top."

"They can be scarcely less than ninety feet," was the reply, "and they are very fine specimens of the family; but the great chestnut which is the only tree in the field on the left of the house is broader. It spreads out like an apple tree, because it has abundance of room, and it is nearly as broad as it is high."

"And aren't its chestnuts just splendid?" exclaimed Malcolm--"the biggest we find anywhere."

"The bark, you see," continued his governess, "is very dark-colored, hard and rugged, with long, deep clefts. In smaller and younger trees it is smooth. I suppose I need not tell you that the fruit is within a burr covered with sharp, stiff bristles which are not handled with impunity. It opens by four valves more than halfway down when ripe, and contains the nuts, from one to three in number, in a downy cup. These green burrs are very ornamental to the tree; and when they are ripe, the green takes on a yellow tinge."

"You didn't say anything about the cunning little tails of the nuts, Miss Harson," said Edith, in a disappointed tone. "I think they're the prettiest part, and they stick up in the burr like little mice-tails."

"Well, dear," was the smiling reply, "you have told us about them, and I think you have given a very good description. That is just what they always reminded me of when I was about your age--little mice-tails."

Edith looked pleased and shy, and she did not mind Malcolm's laughing at her "little tails," because Miss Harson used to think the same as she did about them.

"This beautiful tree came from Asia, and it belongs to the Castanea family, the Greeks having given it that name from a town in Pontus where they obtained it. It was transplanted into the North and West, and is now found in most temperate regions. The wood of the chestnut is very valuable, as it is strong, elastic and durable, and is often used as a substitute for oak and pine. It makes very beautiful furniture."

"What kind of chestnuts," asked Clara, "are those great big ones, like horse-chestnuts, that they have in some of the stores? Are they good to eat?"

"Yes," replied Miss Harson; "they are particularly good, and many people in the southern countries of Europe almost live on them. They are three or four times larger than our nuts, these Spanish and Italian chestnuts, and they are eaten instead of bread and potatoes by the peasantry of Spain and Italy. The Spanish chestnut is one of the most stately of European trees, and sometimes it is found growing in our own country, but never in the woods. It is carefully planted and cultivated as an ornamental tree for private grounds. And now," added the young lady, "as we have sufficiently examined our American chestnut trees and it is rather damp and cool to-day for tent-life, suppose we return to the house and get better acquainted with the foreign chestnuts?"

Edith asked if there was to be a story, but she did not complain when Miss Harson thought not, only an account of a very large tree; for the children always felt quite sure that there would be something which they would like to hear.

* * * * *

The evening was damp, and Clara said that, the schoolroom looked like a mixture of summer and winter. The fire was both pleasant and comfortable, but there were lilacs and tulips and hyacinths and plenty of wild flowers in vases and baskets; the leaves were all out on the trees by the windows, and the grass was like velvet.

"One of the largest trees in the world, if not the largest," said Miss Harson, "is a chestnut tree on the side of Mount Etna, in Sicily, which abounds with chestnut trees of giant proportions and remarkable beauty. It is called 'The Chestnut Tree of a Hundred Horses,' and this title is said to have originated in a report that a queen of Aragon once took shelter under its branches attended by her principal nobility, all of whom found refuge from a violent storm under the spreading boughs of the tree. At one time it was supposed that the tree really consisted of a clump of several united, but this is not the case; for on digging away the earth the root was found entire, and at no great depth. Five enormous branches rise from the trunk, the outside surface of each being covered with bark, while on the inside is none. The verdure and the support of the tree thus depend on the outer bark alone. The intervals between the branches are of various extent, one of them being sufficient to allow two carriages to drive abreast. In the middle cavity--or what is called the hollow--of the tree a hut has been built for the use of persons employed in collecting and preserving the fruit. They dry the chestnuts in an oven, and then make them into various conserves for sale. A whole caravan of men and animals were once accommodated in the enclosure, and also a flock of sheep folded there. The age of this prodigious tree must be very great indeed. It belongs to the tribe which bears sweet, or edible, chestnuts, that form an agreeable article of food. The foliage is rich, shadowy and beautiful.

"The wood of the chestnut is much used in England for hop-poles, and old houses in London are floored or wainscoted with it. The beautiful roof of Westminster Abbey is made of chestnut wood.

"There are magnificent forests of Spanish chestnuts in the Apennines, and it was the favorite tree of the great painter Salvator Rosa, who spent much time studying the beautiful play of light and shade on its foliage. The peasants make a gala-time of gathering and preparing the nuts. A traveler, having penetrated the extensive forest which covers the Vallombrosan Apennines for nearly five miles, came unexpectedly upon those festive scenes, which are not unfrequent among the chestnut-range. It was a holiday, and a group of peasants dressed in the gay and picturesque attire of the neighborhood of the Arno were dancing in an open and level space covered with smooth turf and surrounded with magnificent chestnuts, while the inmost recesses of the forest resounded with their mirth and minstrelsy. Some beat down the chestnuts with sticks and filled baskets with them, which they emptied from time to time; others, stretched listlessly upon the turf, picked out the contents of the bristling capsules in which the kernels were entrenched, for these, when newly gathered, are sweet and nutritious; others again, and especially young peasant-girls, pelted their companions with the fruit."

"Like snowballing," said Malcolm; "only the prickers must have stung. What grand times they had with their chestnuting!"

"These gay, thoughtless people," replied his governess, "almost live in the open air and enjoy the present moment. It is not easy to tell what they would do without these bountiful chestnut-harvests, for their principal article of food is a thick porridge called polenta, which they make from the ground nuts. In France a kind of cake is made from the same material, and the chestnuts are prepared by drying them in smoke. Another dish is like mashed potatoes, and large quantities are exported in the shape of sweetmeats, made by dipping them, after boiling, into clarified sugar and drying them."

"Miss Harson," asked Clara, "why are horse-chestnuts called 'horse-chestnuts'? Do horses like 'em?"

"Not usually," was the reply. "The nuts are sometimes ground and given to horses, but, as sheep, deer and other cattle eat them in their natural state, it would seem more reasonable to name them after some of those animals, if that was the reason. It is likely that because they look like chestnuts, but are much larger, they were called 'horse-chestnuts,' The tree is not in any respect a chestnut; and when it was first planted in England, some centuries ago, it was called 'a rare foreign tree,' and was much admired. It is supposed to have come from India. The large nuts are like chestnuts in appearance.--Except, Edith, that they have no 'cunning little tails.'--In the month of May there is not a more beautiful tree to be found than the horse-chestnut, with its large, deeply-cut leaves of a bright-green color and its long, tapering spikes of variegated flowers, which turn upward from the dense foliage. The tree at this time has been compared to a huge chandelier, and the erect blossoms to so many wax lights. The bitter nuts ripen early in the autumn and fall from the tree, but long before this the beautiful foliage has turned rusty in our Northern States, and is no longer ornamental. The overshadowing branches, which give such a pleasant shade in summer, early in autumn begin to show the ravages of the insects or the natural decay of the leaves."

"Then," said Malcolm, "it isn't a nice tree to have, and I'm glad that there are elms here instead."

"I should like to have some of all the trees," replied Clara, "because then we could study about them better.--Wouldn't you, Miss Harson?"

"I think so," said her governess, "if they were not undesirable to have, as some trees are. If it were always May, I should want horse-chestnut trees; for I think there is scarcely anything so pretty as those fresh leaves and blossoms. The branches, too, begin low down, and that gives the tree a generous spreading look which is very attractive in the way of shade. In more southern States they have a longer season of beauty than those in the North."

"Do people ever eat the horse-chestnut?" asked Edith.

"Not often, dear--it is too bitter; but an old writer who lived in the days when it was first seen in England says that he planted it in his orchard as a fruit tree, between his mulberry and his walnut, and that he roasted the chestnuts and ate them. It is like the bitternut-hickory, which even boys will not eat."

"I should think that somebody or something ought to eat it," said Clara, thoughtfully; "it seems like such a waste."

Everyone laughed at her wise air, and she was asked if she intended to set the example. She was not quite ready, though, to do that; and Miss Harson continued:

"A naturalist once took from the tree a tiny flower-bud and proceeded to dissect it. After the external covering, which consisted of seventeen scales, he came upon the down which protects the flower. On removing this he could perceive four branchlets surrounding the spike of flowers, and the flowers themselves, though so minute, were as distinct as possible, and he could not only count their number, but discern the stamens, and even the pollen."

"Oh!" exclaimed the children; "how very curious!"

"Yes," replied their governess; "it shows how perfect and wonderful, from the beginning, are all the works of God."

CHAPTER XVIII.

AMONG THE PINES.

"How good it smells here!" exclaimed Edith, with her small nose in the air to inhale what she called "a good sniff" in the fragrant pine-woods.

Miss Harson had taken the children in the carriage to a pine-grove some miles from Elmridge, and Thomas and the horses waited by the roadside while the little party walked about or stood gazing up at the tall slender trees that seemed to tower to the very skies. Thomas was not fond of waiting, but he thought that he had the best of it in this case: it was more cheerful to sit in the carriage and "flick" the flies from Rex and Regina than to go poking about in the gloomy pine-woods. Yet, notwithstanding the darkness of its interior and the sombre character of its dense masses of evergreen foliage as seen from without--whence the name of "black timber," which has been applied to it--the shade and shelter it affords and the sentiment of grandeur it inspires cause it to become allied with the most profound and agreeable sensations; and it was something of this feeling, though they could not express it in words, which possessed the young tree-hunters as they stood in the pine-grove.

"It's nice to breathe here," said Clara.

"It is delicious," replied her governess, enthusiastically, her eyes kindling as she repeated the lines:

"'His praise, ye winds, that from four quarter blow, Breathe soft and loud; and wave your tops, ye pines, With every plant, in sign of worship. Wave!'"

"What a queer brown color--almost like red--the ground is!" said Malcolm. "And look, Miss Harson! it's made of lots of little sharp sticks."

"The sharp sticks are pine-needles," was the reply--"the dead pine-leaves of last year; and when the new growth of leaves have been put forth, they cover the ground with a smooth brown matting as comfortable as a gravel-walk, and yet a carpet of Nature's making. 'The foliage of the pine is so hard and durable that in summer we always find the last year's crop lying upon the ground in a state of perfect soundness, and under it that of the preceding year only partially decayed.'"

"It's kind of slippery in some places," continued Malcolm, taking a slide as he spoke. "And see those queer-looking roots sprouting out of the ground!"

"I see the roots," said Miss Harson, "but no sprouts. That is the white pine, the roots of which are often seen above the ground, spreading to some distance from the trunk. Generally the roots of pine trees are small, compared with the size of the trunks, and spread horizontally instead of descending far into the ground. For this reason pines are often uprooted by high winds, which break off the deciduous trees near the ground. But I wish you particularly to notice the trunks of these trees and tell me if you can see any difference in them."

Those particular trees had probably never been stared at so hard before, and the three children exclaimed almost together:

"Some are rough, and some are smooth, and the rough ones have little bunches of leaves on 'em."

"These are the pitch-pines," replied their governess. "They are the roughest of all our forest-trees, and they have a rounder head than any of the other American evergreens. The branches, you see, turn in various directions and are curved downward at the ends. This tree has also the peculiar habit of sending out little branchlets full of leaves along the stem from the root upward, and this has a very pretty effect, like that of some elm trees. It is the pitch-pine that produces the fragrance we are all enjoying so much. What do you notice about the smoother trees?"

"They are very tall and big," replied Clara--"ever so much handsomer than the rough ones."

"The white pine," said Miss Harson, "is one of the loftiest and most valuable of North American trees. Its top can be seen at a great distance, looking like a spire as it towers above the heads of the trees around it. You see that it has widespread branches and silken-looking, tufted foliage. The leaves are in fives and not so stiff as those of the other pines, and you will notice that the branches are in whorls, like a series of stages one above another. The foliage has a tasseled effect with those long silky tufts at the ends of the branches, and the whole outline of the tree is very pleasing."

"This isn't a pine tree, is it?" asked Malcolm, touching a small tree with very slender branches, some of them as slight as willow-withes and covered with grayish-red bark, while that on the main stem was bluish gray.

"It is a species of pine," was the reply, "because it belongs to the Coniferae, or cone-producing, family; but it is not an evergreen, although it ranks as such. This is the larch--generally called in New England by its Indian name of hacmatack--and it differs from the other pines in its crowded tufts of leaves, which, after turning to a soft leather-color, fall, in New England, early in November. The cones, too, are very small."

"What's the use of cones, any way?" asked Malcolm as he picked up some very large ones under the white and pitch pines.

"Their principal use," replied his governess, "is to contain the seeds of future trees: they are the fruit of the pine; but they have a number of uses besides, which you shall hear about this evening."

"The little cones at Hemlock Lodge are pretty," said Edith, "and Clara and me play with 'em. We play they're a orphan-'sylum."

"'Clara and I,' dear," corrected Miss Harson, smiling at the "orphan-'sylum," while Malcolm said he had never thought of that before, and it must be what they were meant for. Edith could not quite understand whether this was fun or earnest, but Miss Harson shook her head at Malcolm and called him "naughty boy."

"The spruce and hemlock," continued their governess, "and many of the other evergreens, we have at Elmridge, but I brought you here to-day for our drive that you might examine these magnificent pine trees, and so be better able to understand whatever we can find out about them this evening. Thomas is probably tired of waiting by this time; so we will leave the fragrant pine-woods for the present, and promise ourselves some future visits."

Every green thing was now in full summer beauty, and daisies and buttercups gemmed the fields, while the garden at Elmridge was all aglow with blossoms, The children remembered their flower-studies of last year, and took fresh pleasure in the woods because of them; but the trees now seemed quite as interesting as the flowers had been.

* * * * *

"The trees known as evergreens," said Miss Harson, "are not so bright and cheerful-looking as those which are deciduous, or leaf-shedding, but they have the advantage of being clothed with foliage, although of a sober hue, all the year round. They consist of pines, firs, junipers, cypresses, spruces, larches, yews and hemlocks, with some foreign trees, and form a distinct and striking natural group. 'This family has claims to our particular attention from the importance of its products in naval, and especially in civil and domestic, architecture, and in many other arts, and, in some instances, in medicine. Some of the species in this country are of more rapid growth, attain to a larger size and rise to a loftier height than any other trees known. The white pine is much the tallest of our native trees.'"

"How high does it grow, Miss Harson?" asked Clara.

"From one hundred and fifty to two hundred feet," was replied, "and on the north-west coast of America one called the 'Douglas's pine' is the loftiest tree known; it is said to measure over three hundred feet. 'From the pines are obtained the best masts and much of the most valuable ship-timber, and in the building and finishing of houses they are of almost indispensable utility. The bark of some of them, as the hemlock and larch, is of great value in tanning, and from others are obtained the various kinds of pitch, tar, turpentine, resin and balsams,' The pines and firs have circles of branches in imperfect whorls around the trunk, and, as one of these whorls is formed each year, it is easy to calculate the age of young trees. In thick woods the lower whorls of branches soon decay for want of light and air, and this leaves a smooth trunk, which rises without a branch, like a beautiful shaft, for a hundred feet or more.

"These trees are found everywhere except in the hot regions around the equator. The white pine is the most common, but in the evergreen woods of our own country it is mixed with pitch-pine and fir trees. In our Southern States there are thin forests, called pine-barrens, through which one can travel for miles on horseback. The white pine is easily distinguished by its leaves being in fives, by its very long cones, composed of loosely-arranged scales, and when young by the smoothness and delicate light-green color of the bark. It is known throughout New England by the name 'white pine,' which is given it on account of the whiteness of the wood. In England it is called the Weymouth pine.

"Many very large trees are found in Maine, on the Penobscot River, but most of the largest and most valuable timber trees have been cut down. The lumberers, as they are called, are constantly hewing down the grand old trees for timber, white pine being the principal timber of New England and Canada."

"And they float it down the rivers on rafts, don't they?" said Malcolm. "Won't you tell us about that, Miss Harson?"

"Yes," was the reply.--"But do not look so expectant, Edie; it is not a story, dear, only a description of pine-cutting in the forests of Maine and Canada. But I should like you to know how these great trees are turned into timber, and you will see that, like many other necessary things, it is neither easy nor pleasant. We do not get much without hard work on the part of somebody: remember that. Now I will read:

"'The business of procuring trees suitable for masts of ships is difficult and fatiguing. The pines which grew in the neighborhood of the rivers and in the most accessible places have all been cut down. Paths have now to be cleared with immense labor to the recesses of the forest, in order to obtain a fresh supply. This arduous employment is called "lumbering," and those who engage in it are "lumberers." The word "lumber," in its general sense, applies to all kinds of timber. But though many different trees, such as oak, ash and maple, are cut down, yet the main business is with the pines. And when a suitable plot of ground has been chosen for erecting a saw-mill,' to prepare the boards, 'it is called "pine-land," or a spot where the pine trees predominate.

"'A body of wood-cutters unite to form what is called a "lumbering-party," and they are in the employ of a master-lumberman, who pays them wages and finds them in provisions. The provisions are obtained on credit and under promise of payment when the timber has been cut down and sold. If the timber meets with any accident in its passage down the river, the master-lumberman cannot make good the loss, and the shopkeeper loses his money.

"'When the lumbering-party are ready to start, they take with them a supply of necessaries, and also what tools they will require, and proceed up the river to the heart of the forest. When they reach a suitable spot where the giant trees which are to serve for masts grow thick and dark, they get all their supplies on shore--their axes, their cooking-utensils and the casks of molasses'--and too often of whisky or rum, too, I am sorry to say--'that will be used lavishly. The molasses is used instead of sugar to sweeten the great draughts of tea--made, not from the product of China, but from the tops of the hemlock.

"'The first thing to be done is to build some kind of shelter, for they must remain in the forest until spring, and the cold of those Northern winters is terrible. Their cabin--for it cannot be called by any better name--is built of logs of wood cut down on purpose and put together as rudely as possible. It is only five feet high, and the roof is covered with boards. There is a great blazing fire kept up day and night, for the frost is intense, and the provisions have to be kept in a deep place made in the ground under the cabin. The smoke of the fire goes out through a hole in the roof, and the floor is strewn with branches of fir, the only couch the poor hardworking lumberers have to rest upon. When night comes, they turn into the cabin to sleep, and lie with their feet to the fire. If a man chances to awaken, he instantly jumps up and throws fresh logs on the fire; for it is of the utmost importance not to let it go out. One of the men is the cook for the whole party, and his duty is to have breakfast ready before it is light in the morning. He prepares a meal of boiled meat and the hemlock tea sweetened with molasses, and the rest of the party partake heartily of both, and in some camps also of rum, under the mistaken notion that it helps them to bear the severe toil. When breakfast is over, they divide into several gangs. One gang cuts down the trees, another saws them in pieces, and the third gang is occupied in conveying them, by means of oxen, to the bank of the nearest stream, which is now frozen over.

"'It is a hard winter for the lumbermen. The snow covers the ground until the middle of May, and the frost is often intense. But they toil through it, felling, sawing and conveying until a quantity of trees have been laid prostrate and made available for the market. Then, at last, the weather changes; the snow begins to melt and the streams and rills are set at liberty. The rivers flow briskly on and are much swollen with the melting snow, and the men say that the freshets have come down.

"'Hard as their toil has been, the most difficult and fatiguing has yet to be encountered. The timber is collected on the banks of the river, and has now to be thrown into the water and made into rafts, so that it can be floated down to the nearest market-town. The water, filled with melting snow, is deadly cold and can scarcely be endured, but the men are in it from morning till night constructing the rafts, which are put together as simply as possible, and the smallest outlay made to suffice. The rafts are of different sizes, according to the breadth of the stream; and when all is ready, they are launched, and the convoy fairly sets out on its voyage.

"'The great ugly masses of floating timber move slowly along under the care of a pilot, and the lumberers ride upon the rafts, often without shelter or protection from the weather. They guide themselves by long and powerful poles fixed on pivots, and which act as rudders. As they journey down the stream they sing and shout and make the utmost noise and riot. If there comes a storm or a change of weather, the pilot steers his convoy into some safe creek for the night, and secures it as best he can.

"'Thus by degrees the raft reaches the place of destination, occasionally with some loss and damage to the timber. In this case the master-lumberer bears the loss, and is obliged to refund the expenses incurred as best he can. At any rate, the men are now paid off, and set out on foot for their homes.'"

Malcolm was particularly delighted with this narrative of stirring activity, and even the little girls seemed very much interested in it. They were so sorry for the poor lumbermen who had such dreary winters off there in the Northern woods, and Clara wondered if they couldn't have warm comforters and mittens.

"They probably have those things when they go into camp," said Miss Harson, "but they are likely to find them in the way of working, and to cast them aside.--Great ships are not built for nothing: even to get the timber in readiness costs heavy labor, but, after all, no doubt, the men get interested in it and enjoy its excitement. Fortunately for the many uses to which its timber is put, the white pine grows very rapidly, gaining from fifteen inches to three feet every year. In deep and damp old woods it is slower of growth; it is then almost without sap-wood and has a yellowish color like the flesh of the pumpkin. For this reason it is called 'pumpkin-pine.' The bark of young trees of the white-pine species is very smooth and of a reddish, bottle-green color. It is covered in summer with a pearly gloss. On old trunks the bark is less rough than that of any other pine. This tree has the spreading habit of the cedar of Lebanon. In addition to its grand and picturesque character, the white pine, says a lover of trees, may be 'regarded as a true symbol of benevolence. Under its outspread roof numerous small animals, nestling in the bed of dry leaves that cover the ground, find shelter and repose. The squirrel feeds upon the kernels obtained from its cones; the hare browses upon the trefoil'--clover--'and the spicy foliage of the hypericum'--St. John's wort--'which are protected in its shade; and the fawn reposes on its brown couch of leaves unmolested by the outer tempest. From its green arbors the quails are often roused in midwinter, where they feed upon the berries of the Mitchella and the spicy wintergreen. Nature, indeed, seems to have specially designed this tree to protect her living creatures both in summer and in winter.'"

"Hurrah for the white pine," said Malcolm, with great energy, "the grand old American tree!"

"I'm glad that the little birds and animals have such a nice home under it in winter," said Clara.

"I'm glad too," added Edith, "but I wish we could find some and see how they look in their soft bed. Don't they ever put their heads out the least bit, Miss Harson?"

"Not when they suspect that there is any one around, dear, and the little creatures are very sharp to find this out. Our heavenly Father, you know, takes thought for sparrows and all such helpless things, and they are fed and cared for without any thought of their own.--The white pine," she continued, "is truly a magnificent tree, but I think we shall find that the pitch-pine is also very useful."

"That's the rough one," said Malcolm; "I remember how it looks, with little tufts sticking out along the trunk."

"Yes," replied his governess, "and out authority says this tree is distinguished by its leaves being in threes--the white pine, you know, has them in fives--by the rigidity and sharpness of the scales of its cones, by the roughness of its bark, and by the denseness of the brushes of its stiff, crowded leaves. Its usual height is from forty to fifty feet, but it is sometimes much taller. The trunk is not only rough, but very dark in color; and from this circumstance the species is frequently called black pine. The wood is very hard and firm, and contains a quantity of resin. This is much more abundant in the branches than in the trunk, and the boards and other lumber of this wood are usually full of pitch-knots."

"What are pitch-knots?" asked Clara.

"'When a growing branch,'" read Miss Harson, "'is broken off, the remaining portion becomes charged with resin,' which is deposited by the resin-bearing sap of the tree, 'forming what is called a pitch-knot, extending sometimes to the heart. The same thing takes place through the whole heart of a tree when, full of juice, its life is suddenly destroyed.' 'Resin' is another name for turpentine, but is used of it commonly when hardened into a solid form. The tar is obtained by slowly burning splintered pine, both trunk and root, with a smothered flame, and collecting the black liquid, which is expelled by the heat and caught in cavities beneath the burning pile. Pitch is thickened tar, and is used in calking ships and for like purposes."

"I am going to remember that," said Malcolm; "I could never make out what all those different things meant."

"What are you thinking about so seriously, Clara?" asked her governess. "If it is a puzzle, let me see if I cannot solve it for you."

"Well, Miss Harson, I was thinking of those brown leaves, or 'needles,' in the pine-woods, and it seems strange to say that the leaves of evergreens never fall off."

"It would not only be strange, dear, but quite untrue, to say that; for the same leaves do not, of course, remain for ever on the tree. The deciduous trees lose their leaves in the autumn and are entirely bare until the next spring, but the evergreens, although they renew their leaves, too, are never left without verdure of some sort. Late in October you may see the yellow or brown foliage of the pines, then ready to fall, surrounding the branches of the previous year's growth, forming a whorl of brown fringe surmounted by a tuft of green leaves of the present year's growth. Their leaves always turn yellow before the fall."

CHAPTER XIX.

GIANT AND NUT PINES.

Great was the surprise of Edith when Miss Harson gave the little sleeper a gentle shake and told her that it was time to be up. But the birds without the window told the same story, and the little maiden was soon at the breakfast-table and ready for the day's duties and enjoyments, including their "tree-talk."

"Are there any more kinds of pine trees?" asked Malcolm.

"Yes, indeed!--more than we can take up this summer," replied Miss Harson. "There is the Norway pine, or red pine, which in Maine and New Hampshire is often seen in forests of white and pitch pine. It has a tall trunk of eighty feet or so, and a smooth reddish bark. The leaves are in twos, six or eight inches long, and form large tufts or brushes at the end of the branchlets. The wood is strong and resembles that of the pitch-pine, but it contains no resin. The giant pines of California belong to a different species from any that we have been considering, and the genus, or order, in which they have been arranged is called Sequoia[19]. They are generally known, however, as the 'Big Trees.' In one grove there are a hundred and three of them, which cover a space of fifty acres, called 'Mammoth-Tree Grove.' One of the giants has been felled--a task which occupied twenty-two days. It was impossible to cut it down, in the ordinary sense of the term, and the men had to bore into it with augers until it was at last severed in twain. Even then the amazing bulk of the tree prevented it from falling, and it still kept its upright position. Two more days were employed in driving wedges into the severed part on one side, thus to compel the giant to totter and fall. The trunk was no less than three hundred and two feet in height and ninety-six in circumference. The stump, which was left standing, presented such a large surface that a party of thirty couples have danced with ease upon it and still left abundant room for lookers-on."

[19] Sequoia gigantea.

When the children had sufficiently exclaimed over the size of this huge tree, their governess continued:

"It is thought that these trees must have been growing for more than two thousand years, which would make them probably two hundred years old at the birth of our Saviour. Does it not seem wonderful to think of? There are other groups of giant pines scattered on the mountains and in the forests, and some youthful giants about five hundred years old."

"I suppose they are the babies of the family," said Clara; and this idea amused Edith very much.

"There is still another kind of pine," said Miss Harson--"the Italian, or stone, pine. It is shaped almost exactly like an umbrella with a very long handle. The Pinus pinea bears large cones, the seed of which is not only eatable, but considered a delicious nut. The cone is three years in ripening; it is then about four inches long and three wide, and has a reddish hue. Each scale of which the cone is formed is hollow at the base and contains a seed much larger than that of any other species. When the cone is ripe, it is gathered by the owners of the forest; and when thoroughly dried on the roof or thrown for a few minutes into the fire, it separates into many compartments, from each of which drops a smooth white nut in shape like the seed of the date. The shell is very hard, and within it is the fruit, which is much used in making sweetmeats. The stone-pine is found also in Palestine, and is supposed to be the cypress of the Bible. The author of The Ride Through Palestine[20] speaks of passing through a fine grove of the stone-pine, 'tall and umbrella-topped,' with dry sticks rising oddly here and there from the very tops of the trees.

These sticks were covered with birdlime, to snare the poor bird which might be tempted to set foot on such treacherous supports; and if the cones were ripe, they would be quite sure to do it. Here is the picture, from the book just mentioned. Italian pine is a prettier name than stone-pine, and this is the name by which it is known to artists, who put it into almost every picture of Italian scenery.

"'Much they admire that old religious tree With shaft above the rest upshooting free, And shaking, when its dark locks feel the wind, Its wealthy fruit with rough and massive rind.'"

[20] Presbyterian Board of Publication.

[Illustration: STONE-PINE--"FIR" (Pinus maritima)].

"But how queer it sounds to call fruit wealthy!" said Malcolm.

"It is odd," replied his governess, "only because the word is not now used in that sense; but the fruit is wealthy both because of its abundance and because it can be put to so many uses. Let us see what is said of it:

"'The kernels, or seeds, from the cones of the stone-pine have always been esteemed as a delicacy. In the old days of Rome and Greece they were preserved in honey, and some of the larders of the ill-fated city of Pompeii were amply stored with jars of this agreeable conserve, which were found intact after all those years. The kernels are also sugared over and used as bonbons. They enter into many dishes of Italian cookery, but great care has to be taken not to expose them to the air. They are usually kept in the cones until they are wanted, and will then retain their freshness for some years. The squirrels eagerly seek after the fruit of this pine and almost subsist upon it. They take the cone in their paws and dash out the seeds, thus scattering many of them and helping to propagate the tree.

"'There is a bird called the crossbill that makes its nest in the pine. It fixes its nest in place by means of the resin of the tree and coats it with the same material, so as to render it impervious to the rain. The seeds from the cones form its chief food, and it extracts them with its curious bill, the two parts of which cross each other. It grasps the cone with its foot, after the fashion of a parrot, and digs into it with the upper part of its bill, which is like a hook, and forces out the seed with a jerk.'"

The children enjoyed this account very much, and they thought that stone-pine nuts--which they had never seen, and perhaps never would see--must be the most delicious nuts that ever grew.

"What nice times the birds have," said Clara, "helping themselves to all the good things that other people can't reach!"

"They are not exactly 'people,'" replied Miss Harson, laughing; "and, in spite of all these 'nice times,' you would not be quite willing to change with them, I think."

No, on the whole, Clara was quite sure that she would not.

CHAPTER XX.

MORE WINTER TREES: THE FIRS AND THE SPRUCES.

There were some beautiful evergreens on the lawn at Elmridge, and, although the foliage seemed dark in summer, it gave the place a very cheerful look in winter, when other trees were quite bare, while the birds flew in and out of them so constantly that spring seemed to have come long before it really did arrive.

"This balsam-fir," said Miss Harson as they stood near a tall, beautiful tree that tapered to a point, "has, you see, a straight, smooth trunk and tapers regularly and rapidly to the top. You will notice, too, that the leaves, which are needle-shaped and nearly flat, do not grow in clusters, but singly, and that their color is peculiar. There are faint white lines on the upper part and a silvery-blue tinge beneath, and this silvery look is produced by many lines of small, shining resinous dots. The deep-green bark, striped with gray, is full of balsam, or resin, known as balm of Gilead or Canada balsam, and highly valued as a cure for diseases of the lungs. The long cones are erect, or standing, and grow thickly near the ends of the upper branches. They have round, bluish-purple scales, and the soft color has a very pretty effect on the tree. They ripen every year, and the lively little squirrel, as he is called, feasts upon them, as the crossbill does on the cones of the stone-pine. But the mischievous little animal also barks the boughs and gnaws off the tops of the leading shoots, so that many trees are injured and defaced by his depredations."

"He is a lively little squirrel," observed Malcolm. "How he does race! But he doesn't gnaw our trees, does he?"

"No, I think not, for he prefers staying in the woods and fields; but fir-woods are his especial delight. Our balsam-fir is the American sister of the silver fir of Europe, both having bluish-green foliage with a silvery under surface, in a single row on either side of the branches, which curve gracefully upward at the ends. The tree has a peculiarly light, airy appearance until it is old, when there is little foliage except at the ends of the branches. The silver fir is one of the tallest trees on the continent of Europe, and it is remarkable for the beauty of its form and foliage and the value of its timber."

"I know what this tree is," said Clara, turning to an evergreen of stately form and graceful, drooping branches that almost touched the ground: "it's Norway spruce. Papa told me this morning."

"Yes," replied her governess, "and a beautiful tree it is, like the fir in many respects, but the bark is rougher and the cones droop. The branches, too, are lower and more sweeping. But the fir and the spruce are more alike than many sisters and brothers. The Scotch fir, about which there are many interesting things to be learned, is more rugged-looking, and the Norway spruce, which will bear studying too, is more grand and majestic."

"I know this one, Miss Harson," said little Edith as they came to a sweeping hemlock near the bay-window of the dining-room.

"Yes, dear," was the reply; "Hemlock Lodge has made you feel very well acquainted with the tree after which it is named. It is one of the most beautiful of the evergreens, with its widely-spreading branches and their delicate, fringe-like foliage; but, although the branches are ornamental for church and house decoration, they are very perishable, and drop their small needles almost immediately when placed in a heated room. And now," continued the young lady, "we have come back to warm piazza-days again, and can have our talk in the open air."

So on the piazza they speedily established themselves, with Miss Harson in the low, comfortable chair and her audience on the crimson cushions that had been piled up in a corner.

"We shall find a great deal about the fir tree," said Miss Harson, "as it is very hardy and rugged, and as common in all Northern regions as the white birch--quite as useful, too, as we shall soon see. This rugged species--which is generally called the Scotch fir--is not so smooth and handsome as our balsam-fir, but it is a tree which the people who live near the great Northern forests of Europe could not easily do without. It belongs to the great pine family and is often called a pine, but in the countries of Great Britain especially it is called the Scotch fir. Although well shaped, it is not a particularly elegant-looking tree. The branches are generally gnarled and broken, and the style of the tree is more sturdy than graceful. The Scotch fir often grows to the height of a hundred feet, and the bark is of a reddish tinge. 'It is one of the most useful of the tribe, and, like the bountiful palm, confers the greatest blessing on the inhabitants of the country where it grows. It serves the peasants of the bleak, barren parts of Sweden and Lapland for food: their scanty supply of meal often runs short, and they go to the pine to eke it out. They choose the oldest and least resinous of the branches and take out the inner bark. They first grind it in a mill, and then mix it with their store of meal; after this it is worked into dough and made into cakes like pancakes. The bark-bread is a valuable addition to their slender resources, and sometimes the young shoots are used as well as the bark. Indeed, so largely is this store of food drawn upon that many trees have been destroyed, and in some places the forest is actually thinned."

"They're as bad as the squirrels," said Malcolm. "But how I should hate to eat such stuff!"

"It may not be so very bad," replied his governess. "Some people think that only white bread is fit to eat, but I think that Kitty's brown bread is rather liked in this family."

The children all laughed, for didn't papa declare--with such a sober face!--that they were eating him out of house and home in brown bread alone?

Kitty, too, pretended to grumble because the plump loaves disappeared so fast, but she said to herself at the same time, "Bless their hearts! let 'em eat: it's better than a doctor's bill."

"A great many other things besides pancakes are made from the tree," continued Miss Harson, "and the fresh green tops furnish very nice carpets."

There was a faint "Oh!" at this, but, after all, it was not so surprising as the cakes had been.

"They are scattered on the floors of houses as rushes used to be in old times in England, and thus they serve as carpet and prevent the mud and dirt that stick to the shoes of the peasants from staining the floor; and when trodden on, the leaves give out a most agreeable aromatic perfume."

"I'd like that part," said Clara.

[Illustration: THE BLUE SPRUCE.]

"But you cannot have one part without taking it all; almost everything, you see, has a pleasant side.--'The peasant finds no limit to the use of the pine. Of its bark he makes the little canoe which is to carry him along the river; it is simple in its construction, and as light as possible. When he comes within safe distance of one of those gushing, foaming cataracts that he meets with in his course, he pushes his canoe to land and carries it on his shoulders until the danger is past; then he launches it again, and paddles merrily onward. Not a single nail is used in his canoe: the planks are tightly secured together by a natural cordage made of the roots of the pine. He splits them of the right thickness, and with very little preparation they form exactly the material he needs.'"

Malcolm evidently had some idea of making a canoe of this kind, but he became discouraged when his governess reminded him that he could not cut down trees, and that his father would prefer having them left standing. It did not seem necessary to speak of any difficulties in the way of putting the boat together.

"Another use for the fir is to light up the poor hut of the peasant. 'He splits up the branches into laths and makes them into torches. If he wants a light, he takes one of the laths and kindles it at the fire; then he fixes it in a rude frame, which serves him for a candlestick. The light is very brilliant while it lasts, but is soon spent, and he is in darkness again. The same use is made of the pine. It is no unusual circumstance, in the Scotch pine-woods, to come upon a tree with the trunk scooped out from each side and carried away: the cottager has been to fetch material for his candles. But this somewhat rough usage does not hurt the tree, and it continues green and healthy.' In our Southern States pine-fat with resin is called lightwood, and is used for the same purpose."

"That's an easy way of getting candles," said Clara.

"Easy, perhaps, compared with the trouble of moulding them," replied Miss Harson, "but I do not think we should fancy either way of preparing them."

"Is there anything to tell about the spruce tree?" asked Malcolm.

"It is too much like the fir," replied his governess, "to have any very distinct character; but there are species here, known as the white and black spruce, besides the hemlock."

But the children thought that hemlock was hemlock: how did it come to be spruce?

"Because it has the family features--leaves solitary and very short; cones pendulous, or hanging, with the scales thin at the edge; and the fruit ripens in a single year. The hemlock-spruce, as it is sometimes called, is, I think, the most beautiful of the family. 'It is distinguished from all the other pines by the softness and delicacy of its tufted foliage, from the spruce by its slender, tapering branchlets and the smoothness of its limbs, and from the balsam-fir by its small terminal cones, by the irregularity of its branches and the gracefulness of its whole appearance.' The delicate green of the young trees forms a rich mass of verdure, and at this season each twig has on the end a tuft of new leaves yellowish-green in color and making a beautiful contrast to the darker hue of last year's foliage. The bark of the trunk is reddish, and that of the smooth branches and small twigs is light gray. The branchlets are very small, light and slender, and are set irregularly on the sides of the small branches; so that they form a flat surface. This arrangement renders them singularly well adapted to the making of brooms--a use of the hemlock familiar to housekeepers in the country towns throughout New England. The leaves, which are extremely delicate and of a silvery whiteness on the under side, are arranged in a row on each side of the branchlets. The slender, thread-like stems on which they grow make them move easily with the slightest breath of wind, and this, with the silvery hue underneath, gives to the foliage a glittering look that is very pretty. But I think you all can tell me when the hemlock is prettiest?"

"After a snow-storm," said Clara. "Don't we all look, almost the first thing, at the tree by the dining-room window?"

"Yes," replied Miss Harson; "it is a beautiful sight with the snow lying on it in masses and the dark green of the leaves peeping through. 'The branches put forth irregularly from all parts of the trunk, and lie one above another, each bending over at its extremities upon the surface of those below, like the feathers upon the wings of a bird,' And soft, downy plumes they look, with the snow resting on them and making them more feathery than ever."

"So they are like feathers?" said Malcolm, to whom this was a new idea, "I'll look for 'em the next time it snows; yet--" He was going to add that he wished it would snow to-morrow; but remembering that it was only the beginning of June, and that Miss Harson had shown them how each season has its pleasures, he stopped just in time.

"The pretty little cones of the hemlock, which grow very thickly on the tree, have a crimson tinge at first, and turn to a light brown. They are found hanging on the ends of the small branches, and they fall during the autumn and winter. This tree is a native of the coldest parts of North America, where it is found in whole forests, and it flourishes on granite rocks on the sides of hills exposed to the most violent storms. The wood is firm and contains very little resin; it is much used for building-purposes. A great quantity of tannin is obtained from the bark; and when mixed with that of the oak, it is valuable for preparing leather.

"We have taken the prettiest of the spruces first," continued Miss Harson, "and now we must see what are the differences between them. 'The two species of American spruce, the black and the white--or, as they are more commonly called, the double and the single--are distinguished from the fir and the hemlock in every stage of growth by the roughness of the bark on their branches, produced by little ridges running down from the base of each leaf, and by the disposition of the leaves, which are arranged in spirals equally on every side of the young shoots. The double is distinguished from the single spruce by the darker color of the foliage--whence its name of black spruce--by the greater thickness, in proportion to the length, of the cones, and by the looseness of its scales, which are jagged, or toothed, on the edge.' It is a well-proportioned tree, but stiff-looking, and the dark foliage, which never seems to change, gives it a gloomy aspect. The leaves are closely arranged in spiral lines. The black spruce is never a very large tree, but the wood is light, elastic and durable, and is valuable in shipbuilding, for making ladders and for shingles. The young shoots are much in demand for making spruce-beer. The white spruce is more slender and tapering, and the bark and leaves are lighter. The root is very tough, and the Canadian Indians make threads from the fibres, with which they sew together the birch-bark for their canoes. The wood is as valuable as that of the black spruce."

"Does the Norway spruce come from Norway?" asked Clara.

"Yes; that is its native land, where it presents its most grand and beautiful appearance. There it 'rivals the palm in stature, and even attains the height of one hundred and eighty feet. Its handsome branches spread out on every side and clothe the trunk to its base, while the summit of the tree ends in an arrow-like point. In very old trees the branches droop at the extremities, and not only rest upon the ground, but actually take root in it and grow. Thus a number of young trees are often seen clustering around the trunk of an old one.'"

"Why, that's like the banyan tree," said Malcolm.

"Only there is a difference in the manner of growth, for the branches of the banyan are some distance from the ground and send forth rootlets without touching it. The Norway spruce is also the great tree of the Alps, where it seems to match the majestic scenery. The timber is valuable for building; and when sawed into planks, it is called white deal, while that of the Scotch fir is red deal.

"And now," said Miss Harson, "before we leave the firs, let us see what is said about them in the Bible. They were used for shipbuilding in the city of Tyre; for the prophet Ezekiel says, 'They have made all thy ship boards of fir trees of Senir[21],' and it is written that 'David and all the house of Israel played before the Lord on all manner of instruments made of firwood[22].' The same wood was used then in building houses, as you will find, Malcolm, by turning to the Song of Solomon, seventh chapter, seventeenth verse."

[21] Ezek. xxvii. 5.

[22] 2 Sam. vi. 5.

"'The beams of our house are cedar, and our rafters of fir,'" read Malcolm.

"In Kings it is said, 'So Hiram gave Solomon cedar trees and fir trees, according to his desire[23],' and these trees were to be used for the very house, or palace, of which the Jewish king speaks in his Song. Evergreens are often mentioned in the Bible, and in that beautiful Christmas chapter, the sixtieth of Isaiah, you will find the fir tree again.--Read the thirteenth verse, Clara."

[23] I Kings v. 10.

"'The glory of Lebanon shall come unto thee, the fir tree, the pine tree, and the box together, to beautify the place of my sanctuary; and I will make the place of my feet glorious.'--What is 'the glory of Lebanon,' Miss Harson?"

"The cedar of Lebanon, dear; and we will now turn our attention to that and the other cedars."

CHAPTER XXI.

THE CEDARS.

"The cypress tribe," said Miss Harson, "differ from the pines, or Coniferae, by not having their fruit in a true cone, but in a roundish head which consists of a small number of scales, sometimes forming a sort of berry. One of the most common of this family is the arbor vitae, or tree of life--a tree so small as to look like a pointed shrub, and more used for fences than for ornament. An arbor-vitae hedge, you know, divides our flower garden from the kitchen-garden and goes all the way down to the brook."

"I like the smell of it," said Clara. "Don't you, Miss Harson?"

"Yes," was the reply, "there is something very fresh and pleasant about it; and when well kept, as John is sure to keep ours, it makes a beautiful hedge. As a tree it has been known to reach forty or fifty feet in height, with a trunk ten feet in circumference. The leaves are arranged in four rows, in alternately opposite pairs, and seem to make up the fan-like branchlets. These branchlets look like parts of a large compound, flat leaf. The bark is slightly furrowed, smooth to the touch, and very white when the tree stands exposed. The wood is reddish, somewhat odorous, very light, soft and fine-grained. In the northern part of the United States and in Canada it holds the first place for durability."

"I thought the cypress was a flower," said Malcolm.

"So one kind of cypress is," replied his governess--"the blossom of an airy-looking and beautiful creeper; but the name also belongs to a family of trees. The white cedar, or cypress, is a very graceful tree which generally grows in swamps. 'It is entirely free from the stiffness of the pines, and to the spiry top of the poplar it unites the airy lightness of the hemlock. The trunk is straight and tall, tapering very gradually, and toward the top there are short irregular branches, forming a small but beautiful head, above which the leading shoot waves like a slender plume.' The leaves are very small and scale-like, with sharp points, and grow in four rows on the ends of the branchlets, giving them the appearance of large compound leaves. The wood is very durable, and is used for many building-purposes. It is generally of a faint rose-color, and always keeps its aromatic odor."

"Is that what our cedar-chests are made of to keep the moths from our winter clothes?" asked Clara.

"Yes," replied Miss Harson, "but the name 'cedar' is; not correct, though it is one commonly given to this tree. The wood of the European cypress is also used for many purposes where strength and durability are required, for it really seems never to wear out. This tree is described as tapering and cone-like, with upright branches growing close to the trunk, and in its general appearance a little resembling a poplar. Its frond-like branches are closely covered with very small sharp-pointed leaves of a yellow-green color, smooth and shining, and they remain on the tree five or six years. The cypress is often seen in burying-grounds in Europe, and in Turkey it often stands at each end of a grave. The oldest tree in Europe is thought to be an Italian cypress said to have been planted in the year of our Saviour's birth; it is an object of great reverence in the neighborhood. This ancient tree is a hundred and twenty feet high and twenty-three feet around the trunk.

"The juniper--or red cedar, as it is improperly called--is not a handsome tree, but it is a very useful one. It has a scraggy, stunted look, and the foliage is apt to be rusty; but it will grow in rocky, sandy places where no other tree would even try to hold up its head, and the wood, when made into timber, lasts for a great many years. Posts for fences are made of the juniper or red cedar, and the shipbuilder, boatbuilder, carpenter, cabinet-maker and turner are all steady customers for it. The 'cedar-apples' found on this tree are one phase of the life of a very curious fungus. They are covered with a reddish-brown bark; and when fresh, they are tough and fleshy, somewhat like an unripe apple. When dry they become of a woody nature."

"They pucker up your mouth awfully," said Malcolm, who had made several attempts to eat them; but, do what he would, he could not even "make believe" they were nice.

"I have no doubt of it," was the reply, "remembering the dreadful faces I have seen on some of our rambles. But the birds like them, as they do everything of the kind that is not poisonous."

* * * * *

"Isn't it beautiful?" exclaimed the children, in delight. They were admiring a magnificent cedar of Lebanon in one of the pictures which Miss Harson had collected for their benefit, and it seemed no wonder that the grand spreading tree should be called "the glory of Lebanon."

"It is indeed beautiful," replied their governess; "and think of seeing a whole mountain covered with such trees! A traveler speaks of them as the most solemnly impressive trees in the world, and says that their massive trunks, clothed with a scaly texture almost like the skin of living animals and contorted with all the irregularities of age, may well have suggested those ideas of royal, almost divine, strength and solidity which the sacred writers ascribe to them.--Turn to the ninety-second psalm, Clara, and read the twelfth verse."

"'The righteous shall flourish like the palm tree; he shall grow like a cedar in Lebanon.'"

"In the thirty-first chapter of Ezekiel," continued Miss Harson, "it is written, 'Behold, the Assyrian was a cedar in Lebanon with fair branches, and with a shadowing shroud, and of an high stature; and his top was among the thick boughs. The waters made him great, the deep set him up on high with her rivers running round about his plants, and sent out her little rivers unto all the trees of the field. Therefore his height was exalted above all the trees of the field and his boughs were multiplied, and his branches became long because of the multitude of waters, when he shot forth. All the fowls of heaven made their nests in his boughs, and under his branches did all the beasts of the field bring forth their young, and under his shadow dwelt all great nations.'"

"Are the leaves like those of our cedar trees?" asked Malcolm, who was studying the picture quite intently. "The tree doesn't look like 'em."

"They are somewhat like them," replied his governess, "being slender and straight and about an inch long. They grow in tufts, and in the centre of some of the tufts there is a small cone which is very pretty and often brought to this country by travelers for their friends at home. In The Land and the Book there is a picture of small branches with cones, and the author says of the cedar: 'There is a striking peculiarity in the shape of this tree which I have not seen any notice of in books of travel. The branches are thrown out horizontally from the parent trunk. These again part into limbs, which preserve the same horizontal direction, and so on down to the minutest twigs; and even the arrangement of the clustered leaves has the same general tendency. Climb into one, and you are delighted with a succession of verdant floors spread around the trunk and gradually narrowing as you ascend. The beautiful cones seem to stand upon or rise out of this green flooring.' The same writer says that by examining the different growths of wood inside the trunk of one of the trees these ancient cedars of Lebanon have been proved to be three thousand five hundred years old."

"Oh, Miss Harson!" exclaimed her audience; "could any tree be as old as that?"

"It is possible. The circle of growing wood which is made each year is a pretty good method of telling the age of a tree, and these cedars of Lebanon are considered the oldest trees in the world. Travelers have always spoken of the beauty and symmetry of these trees, with their widespreading branches and cone-like tops. All through the Middle Ages a visit to the cedars of Lebanon was regarded by many persons in the light of a pilgrimage. Some of the trees were thought to have been planted by King Solomon himself, and were looked upon as sacred relics. Indeed, the visitors took away so many pieces from the bark that it was feared the trees would be destroyed. The cedars stand in a valley a considerable way up the mountain, where the snow renders it inaccessible for part of the year."

"Are the trees just in one particular place, then?" asked Malcolm. "I thought they grew all over that country?"

"The principal and best-known grove of very large and ancient cedars of Lebanon is found in one place," replied his governess, "but there are other groves now known to exist. The famous grove was fast disappearing, until there were but few of them left. The pilgrims who went to visit them in such numbers in olden times were accompanied by monks from a monastery about four miles below, who would beseech them not to injure a single leaf. But the greatest care could not preserve the trees. Some of them have been struck down by lightning, some broken by enormous loads of snow, and others torn to fragments by tempests. Some have even been cut down with axes like any common tree. But better care is now taken of them; so that we may hope that the grove will live and increase."

"But why weren't they saved," asked Clara, "when people thought so much of them?"

"It seems to be a part of the general desolation of the land of God's chosen but rebellious people. In the third chapter of the prophet Isaiah, verses eleven and twelve, it is said, 'For the day of the Lord of hosts shall be upon every one that is proud and lofty, and upon every one that is lifted up; and he shall be brought low; and upon all the cedars of Lebanon, that are high and lifted up, and upon all the oaks of Bashan.' The same prophet says, in the tenth chapter and nineteenth verse, 'And the rest of the trees of his forest shall be few, that a child may write them.' These words have been particularly applied to the stately cedars of Lebanon, for 'the once magnificent grove is but a speck on the mountain-side. Many persons have taken it in the distance for a wood of fir trees, but on approaching nearer and taking a closer view the cedars resume somewhat of their ancient majesty. The space they cover is not more than half a mile, but, once amidst them, the beautiful fan-like branches overhead, the exquisite green of the younger trees and the colossal size of the older ones fill the mind with interest and admiration. Within the grove all is hushed as in a land of the past. Where once the Tyrian workman plied his axe and the sound of many voices came upon the ear, there are now the silence and solitude of desertion and decay.'--Malcolm," added his governess, "you may read us what is written in the sixth verse of the fourteenth chapter of Hosea."

"'His branches,'" read Malcolm, "'shall spread, and his beauty shall be as the olive tree, and his smell as Lebanon.' What does that mean, Miss Harson?"

"It means the fragrant resin which exudes from both the trunk and the cones of the beautiful cedar. It is soft, and its fragrance is like that of the balsam of Mecca. 'Everything about this tree has a strong balsamic odor, and hence the whole grove is so pleasant and fragrant that it is delightful to walk in it. The wood is peculiarly adapted for building, because it is not subject to decay, nor is it eaten of worms. It was much used for rafters and for boards with which to cover houses and form the floors and ceilings of rooms. It was of a red color, beautiful, solid and free from knots. The palace of Persepolis, the temple of Jerusalem and Solomon's palace were all in this way built with cedar, and the house of the forest of Lebanon was perhaps so called from the quantity of this wood used in its construction.' We are told in First Kings that Solomon 'built also the house of the forest of Lebanon[24],' and that 'he made three hundred shields of beaten gold' and 'put them in the house of the forest of Lebanon[25].' All the drinking-vessels, too, of this wonderful palace, which is always spoken of as 'the house of the forest of Lebanon,' were of pure gold, and its magnificence shows how highly the beautiful cedar-wood was valued."

[24] I Kings vii. 2.

[25] I Kings x. 17.

CHAPTER XXII.

THE PALMS.

"There is a wonderful evergreen," said Miss Harson, "which grows in tropical countries, and also in some sub-tropical countries, such as the Holy Land, and is said to have nearly as many uses as there are days in a year. You must tell me what it is when you have seen the picture."

[Illustration: PALM TREE.]

Malcolm and Clara both pronounced it a palm tree, and Clara asked if there were any such trees growing in this country.

"Some of its relations are found on our Southern seacoast," replied their governess; "South Carolina, you know, is called 'the Palmetto State.' There is a member of the family called the cabbage-palmetto, the unexpanded leaves of which are used as a table vegetable, which you may see in Florida. Its young leaves are all in a mass at the top, and when boiled make a dish something like cabbage. The leaves of the palmetto are also used, when perfect, in the manufacture of hats, baskets and mats, and for many other purposes. But its stately and majestic cousin, the date-palm of the East, with its tall, slender stalk and magnificent crown of feathery leaves, has had its praises sung in every age and clime. 'Besides its great importance as a fruit-producer, it has a special beauty of its own when the clusters of dates are hanging in golden ripeness under its coronal of dark-green leaves. Its well-known fruit affords sustenance to the dwellers on the borders of the great African desert; it is as necessary to them as is the camel, and in many cases they may be said to owe their existence to it alone. The tree rears its column-like stem to the height of ninety feet, and its crown consists of fifty leaves about twelve feet in length and fringed at the edges like a feather. Between the leaf and the stem there issue several horny spathes, or sheaths, out of which spring clusters of panicles that bear small white flowers,' These flowers are followed by the dates, which grow in a dense bunch that hangs down several feet."

"But how do people manage to climb such a tree as that," asked Malcolm, "to get the dates? It goes straight up in the air without any branches, and looks as if it would snap in two if any one tried it."

"It does not snap, though, for it is very strong; and the climbing is easier than you imagine, even when the tree is a hundred feet high, as it sometimes is. The trunk, you see, is full of rugged knots. These projections are the remains of decayed leaves which have dropped off when their work was done. As the older leaves decay the stalk advances in height. It has not true wood, like most trees, but the stem has bundles of fibres that are closely pressed together on the outer part. Toward the root these are so entwined that they become as hard as iron and are very difficult to cut. The tree grows very slowly, but it lives for centuries. I have a Persian fable in rhyme for you, called

'"THE GOURD AND THE PALM.

'""How old art thou?" said the garrulous gourd As o'er the palm tree's crest it poured Its spreading leaves and tendrils fine, And hung a-bloom in the morning shine. "A hundred years," the palm tree sighed.-- "And I," the saucy gourd replied, "Am at the most a hundred hours, And overtop thee in the bowers."

'"Through all the palm tree's leaves there went A tremor as of self-content. "I live my life," it whispering said, "See what I see, and count the dead; And every year of all I've known A gourd above my head has grown And made a boast like thine to-day, Yet here I stand; but where are they?"'"

The children were very much pleased with the fable, and they began to feel quite an affection for the venerable and useful palm tree.

"The date tree," continued their governess, "as this species of palm is often called, blossoms in April, and the fruit ripens in October. Each tree produces from ten to twelve bunches, and the usual weight of a bunch is about fifteen pounds. It is esteemed a crime to fell a date tree or to supply an axe intended for that purpose, even though the tree may belong to an enemy. The date-harvest is expected with as much anxiety by the Arab in the oasis as the gathering in of the wheat and corn in temperate regions. If it were to fail, the Arabs would be in danger of famine. The blessings of the date-palm are without limit to the Arab. Its leaves give a refreshing shade in a region where the beams of the sun are almost insupportable; men, and also camels, feed upon the fruit; the wood of the tree is used for fuel and for building the native huts; and ropes, mats, baskets, beds, and all kinds of articles, are manufactured from the fibres of the leaves. The Arab cannot imagine how a nation can exist without date-palms, and he may well regard it as the greatest injury that he can inflict upon his enemy to cut down his trees."

"Miss Harson," asked Edith, very earnestly, "isn't the palm tree in the Bible?"

[Illustration: DATE-PALM AT JERICHO.]

"It certainly is, dear," replied her governess, "and it is one of the trees most frequently mentioned. In Deuteronomy, thirty-fourth chapter, third verse, Jericho is called the 'city of palm trees.' Travelers still speak of these trees as yet growing in Palestine, but they are not nearly so abundant as they once were; near Jericho only one or two can be found. There are many allusions to the palm in the Scriptures. King David, in the ninety-second psalm, says that the righteous shall flourish like the palm tree: 'Those that be planted in the house of the Lord shall flourish in the courts of our God. They shall bring forth fruit in old age.' The palm is always upright, in spite of rain or wind. 'There it stands, looking calmly down upon the world below, and patiently yielding its large clusters of golden fruit from generation to generation. It brings forth fruit in old age.' The allusion to being planted in the house of the Lord is probably drawn from the custom of planting beautiful and long-lived trees in the courts of temples and palaces. Solomon covered all the walls of the holy of holies round about with golden palm trees.--You will find this, Clara, in First Kings."

Clara read:

"'And he carved all the walls of the house round about with carved figures of cherubim and palm trees and open flowers, within and without[26].'"

[26] I Kings vi. 29.

"In the thirty-second verse," continued Miss Harson, "it is written that he overlaid them with gold, 'and spread gold upon the cherubim, and upon the palm trees.' 'They were thus planted, as it were, within the very house of the Lord; and their presence there was not only ornamental, but appropriate and highly suggestive--the very best emblem not only of patience in well-doing, but of the rewards of the righteous, a fat and flourishing old age, a peaceful end, a glorious immortality.'"

"What does a 'palmer' mean, Miss Harson?" asked Malcolm. "Is it a man who has palm trees or who sells dates? I saw the word in a book I was reading, but I couldn't understand what it meant."

"In olden times," replied his governess, "when people made so many pilgrimages, some of the pilgrims went to the Holy Land and some to Rome and other places; but those who went to Palestine were thought to be the most devout, both because it was so much farther off and because there were so many sacred spots to visit there. These pilgrims always brought home with them branches of palm, to show that they had really been to the land where the tree grew; and so they were called palmers. To say that such-a-one was a palmer was far more than to say that he was a pilgrim."

"Miss Harson," said Clara, holding up one of the books, "here is a picture called 'the cocoanut-palm,' but I didn't know that cocoanuts grew on palm trees. Will you tell us something about it?"

"Certainly I will, dear," was the reply. "I fully intended to do so, for the cocoanut-palm is too valuable a member of the family to be passed over. This species does not grow in Palestine, and it is not one of the trees of the Bible; its home is in the warmest countries, and it grows most luxuriantly in the islands of the tropics or near the seacoast on the main-lands. Although its general form is similar to that of the date-palm, the foliage and fruit are quite different. The leaves are very much broader, and they have not the light, airy look of the foliage of the date-palm. But 'the cocoanut-palm is the most valuable of Nature's gifts to the inhabitants of those parts of the tropics where it grows, and its hundred uses, as they are not inaptly called, extend beyond the tropics over the civilized world. The beautiful islands of the southern seas are fringed with cocoanut-palms that encircle them as with a green and feathery belt. The ripe nuts drop into the sea, but, protected by their husks, they float away until the tide washes them on to the shore of some neighboring island, where they can take root and grow.'"

"Wouldn't it be nice," said Edith, "if some would float here?"

"A great many cocoanuts float here in ships," replied Miss Harson, "but they would not take root and grow, because the climate is not suited to them; it is too cold for them. We cannot have tropical fruit without tropical heat, and I am sure that none of us would want such a change as that. You may sometimes see small cocoanut trees in hothouses or horticultural gardens, where they are shielded from our cold air. The island of Ceylon, in the East Indies, is full of cocoanut-palm trees, for they are carefully cultivated by the inhabitants, and the feathery groves stretch mile after mile. The tree shoots up a column-like stem to the height of a hundred feet, and is crowned with a tuft of broad leaves about twelve feet long. The flowers are yellowish white and grow in clusters, and the seed ripens into a hard nut which in its fibrous husk is about the size of an infant's head."

"I've seen the nut in its husk," said Malcolm, "when papa took me down to the wharf where the ships come in. There were lots of cocoanuts, and some of 'em had their coats on."

"This brown husk," continued his governess, "is a valuable part of the nut, for the toughest ropes and cables are made of its fibres, as well as the useful brown matting so generally used to cover offices and passages. Brushes, nets and other domestic articles are also manufactured from the husk. Scarcely any other tree in the world is so useful to man or contributes so much to his comfort as the cocoanut-palm. Food and drink are alike obtained from it. The kernel of the nut is an article of diet, and can be prepared in many ways. The native is almost sustained by it, and in Ceylon it forms a part of nearly every dish. The spathe that encloses the yet-unopened flowers is made to yield a favorite beverage called palm-wine, or, more familiarly, 'toddy.' When the fresh juice is used, it is an innocent and refreshing drink; but when left to ferment, it intoxicates, and is the one evil result from the bountiful gifts of the tree. Oil is prepared in great quantities from the nuts and used for various purposes."

"Are there any more kinds of palm trees?" asked the children.

"Yes," was the reply; "there are a great many members of this most useful family, but the one that will interest you most, after the date-and cocoanut-palm, is, I think, the sago-palm."

[Illustration: YOUNG COCOANUT TREE IN POT (Cocos nucifera).]

"Why, Miss Harson!" exclaimed Clara, in surprise; "does sago really grow on a tree?"

"It really grows in a tree--for it is a kind of starch secreted by the tree for the use of its flowers and fruit--and in order to obtain it the tree has to be cut down. The pith is then taken out and cut in slices, soaked in water and roasted; and when it assumes the shape of the small globules in which we see it, it is ready for exportation."

"Well!" said Malcolm; "I never knew that before. We've learned ever so many things, Miss Harson."

"There is one thing about the palm," said Miss Harson, "which I have purposely left for the last--especially as it is the last also of our trees for the present--and that is the sacred associations which its branches have for both Jews and Christians. The Jews were commanded on the first day of the feast of tabernacles to 'take the boughs of goodly trees, branches of palm trees, and the boughs of thick trees, and willows of the brook, to rejoice before the Lord their God.' The palm was a symbol of victory, and branches of it were strewn in the path of conquerors, more especially of those who had fought for religious truth. It is the emblem of the martyr, as a conqueror through Christ. The Sunday before Easter is called Palm Sunday because in the ancient churches leaves of palm were carried that day by worshipers in memory of those strewn in the way on the triumphal entry of the King of Zion into

Jerusalem. You will find it, Malcolm, in John."

Malcolm read very reverently:

"'On the next day, much people that were come to the feast, when they heard that Jesus was coming to Jerusalem, took branches of palm trees, and went forth to meet him, and cried, Hosanna; Blessed is the King of Israel that cometh in the name of the Lord[27].'"

[27] John xii. 12, 13.

"Here," said Miss Harson, "is a little hymn written on these very verses:

"'See a small procession slowly Toward the temple wind its way; In the midst rides, meek and lowly, One whom angel-hosts obey.

"'How the shouting crowd adore him, Now, for once, they know their King; Some their garments cast before him, Green palm-branches others bring.

"'Calmly, yet with holy sorrow, Christ permits the sacrifice. Knowing well that on the morrow Changed will be those fickle cries.

* * * * *

"'Children, when in prayers and praises Loudly we with lips adore, While the heart no anthem raises, Are not we like those of yore?

"'O Lord Jesus, let us never Lift the voice in heartless songs; Help us to remember ever All that to thy name belongs.'"

www.ingramcontent.com/pod-product-compliance
Lightning Source LLC
Chambersburg PA
CBHW071042290526
45795CB00004B/1281